FACING SOCIAL JUSTICE IN SPORTS

THE FACING PROJECT

EDITED BY DR. ADAM J. KUBAN

THE FACING PROJECT PRESS

An imprint of The Facing Project

Muncie, Indiana 47305

facingproject.com

First published in the United States of America by The Facing Project Press, an imprint of The Facing Project and division of The Facing Project Gives Inc., 2022.

First paperback edition September 2022

Cover design by Shantanu Suman

Photos on pages 45 and 46 were provided by storytellers and used with permission.

Library of Congress Control Number: 2022939934

ISBN: 979-8-9860961-0-0 (paperback)

ISBN: 979-8-9860961-1-7 (eBook)

Printed in the United States of America

10 9 8 7 6 5 4 3 2 1

PRAISE FOR FACING SOCIAL JUSTICE IN SPORTS

I've always believed sports can serve as an incredible tool for inspiration and learning. Lessons learned, both as athletes and fans, can make us better. This book – Facing Social Justice in Sports – is literally a textbook example. Reading these stories was eye-opening and instructive, and I couldn't give this book any higher praise.

Don Yaeger
11-time *New York Times* best-selling author

Facing Social Justice in Sports offers a unique, penetrating portrait of athletes as they consider important social issues of our day from sexism to racism to pay equity to violence and more. And it does so through the real voices and emotions and experiences of a diverse group of men and women, presented in a narrative form that effectively engages the reader in insightful conversations with these rare and talented competitors.

Gene Policinski
Former Managing Editor/Sports, *USA TODAY*

From breaking color barriers to shattering glass ceilings, the writers behind Facing Social Justice in Sports provide a deeply thought-provoking and introspective look into the athlete's role as a modern-day cultural disrupter. The collection of writings is purposeful, serving as terrific starting points for dissecting the intersection between sport and great societal concerns. It's a must-read deep dive for any macro-minded sports fan.

Brandon Pope
TV host, writer, and columnist
(Chicago's CW26 TV station; WGN Radio; *Ebony Magazine*; *Chicago Sun-Times*)

Professor Kuban and his students illuminate the flashpoint intersection of sport and activism. What causes someone in the sports world to find their voice and speak for a cause? Is it a lightning-bolt event or an accumulation of experiences from being "the only one" on the team that motivates them to act? Will reading about their experiences create an empathy, an understanding, about their positions on social justice? The answers are in these personal stories — sometimes deeply emotional; sometimes shockingly stark — told to journalism students who help the subjects of this project articulate how they became engaged and how they moved beyond courts and fields to the social arena.

Michael Smith
Retired Director of the Media Management Center
Northwestern University

Facing Social Justice in Sports gives us an on-the-ground account of how athletes are navigating some of the most pressing issues of our day. It's a profoundly human take on sports and society that lets the athletes speak for themselves — in all their humanness and complexity.

Dr. Jackson Bartlett
Associate Director,
Center for the Advancement of Teaching Excellence
University of Illinois-Chicago

iv

Athletes are just as human as the fans in the stadium. The same goes for the people who support them. Everyone brings their experiences, history, hopes, fears, and dreams to the game. And the great thing about sports is how it can bring people of different backgrounds together.

Facing Social Justice in Sports is penned by talented up-and-coming writers at Ball State University, and it's an insightful look at how sports figures grapple with the crucial issues of our day. There's an awful lot to think about in here.

Jon Seidel
Federal Courts Reporter, *Chicago Sun-Times*

With such a wide array of perspectives, Facing Social Justice in Sports furthers the conversation on the roles that athletes play in social-justice movements and gives the reader an opportunity to think critically about the world around them. With each story, I was transported into the minds of folks at the forefront of their respective discipline and was given an opportunity to understand on a deeper level just how important each person is to a movement. Simply brilliant.

Robbie Williford
Associate Director of Residence Life, University of Indianapolis
Co-Founder, Brave the Cycle

I'm a big fan of Facing Social Justice in Sports. It's engaging; it's diverse, and it's not dominated by one sport or aspect of the 'social-justice spectrum.' I think the voices and sources used are interesting and thoughtful.

Jake Bartelson
Sports Reporter, *Kane County Chronicle*

Facing Social Justice in Sports is an oral history project that tackles an important contemporary issue: how athletes and coaches feel about injustice. Kuban's band of college students re-tell the first-person stories of athletes and coaches. And this book is not just limited to the American scene; rather, Kuban deftly includes the stories of international storytellers as well. Another neat facet is the inclusion

v

of a sports writer's perspective on the protest movement started by San Francisco 49er quarterback Colin Kaepernick. Furthermore, there is a diversity of sports represented here — not just football and basketball. These stories are not in your face, yet they make it clear that we as a society need to face up to social justice and come to terms that many of our greatest athletes come from a very different world than most of us fans. What StoryCorps is to general history this Facing Project volume is to the study of societal issues and sports. It is a great complement to John Feinstein's 2021 "Raise a Fist, Take a Knee."

Dr. David W. Bulla
Professor and Chair of the Department of Communication
Pamplin College of Arts, Humanities & Social Sciences
Augusta University (Georgia)

CONTENTS

INTRODUCTION

Dr. Adam J. Kuban, Editor, *Facing Social Justice in Sports*
J.R. Jamison, Co-Founder and President, The Facing Project

Social Justice. It's become a loaded concept, and it's one that means something different to different people, which can make it difficult to define.

Is it a product or a process? Or both?

Is it meant to unify or divide?

If you identify as liberal, is it a rallying cry?

If you identify as conservative, is it a woke buzzword?

Or if you maintain apolitical views, is it just another sociocultural distraction?

We can't govern your interpretation, but we can hope that the mere inclusion of "social justice" in the title doesn't automatically diminish the value of the people featured in this book or their respective stories because that's what this is about — stories — capturing the lived experiences from individuals who run the gamut of sports and the defining moments that propelled them to use their platforms for change.

In the pages that follow, we have athletes, coaches, and sports-media professionals. We have stories from different "tiers" or levels of sports that range from youth to collegiate to pro. Most are domestic, U.S.-based stories, but there are at least two international ones as well. The sports represented include football, baseball, softball, basketball, volleyball, tennis, soccer, lacrosse, swimming, boxing, and racing.

And the topics discussed in these stories, and within the context of these sports, include race/race relations, gender equality, poverty, international-student rights, mental health, disability, and LGBTQ+ challenges.

After the Foreword, the first chapter has a more traditional, journalistic feel to it, as it's based on a (somewhat) current event that's likely in every reader's memory even if they aren't sports aficionados. After that, though, the stories/chapters occur in first-person narrative format, indicative of The Facing Project's empathy model that seeks to create a more understanding world through stories that inspire awareness and action.

And that's the overarching goal of this book: Empathy. To learn what it's like through another's lived experience.

Additionally, the authors in the subtitles of each story/chapter are undergraduate students who enrolled in the intermediate Sports Reporting & Writing course at Ball State University in Indiana. Over the duration of two academic semesters — Spring 2021 and Fall 2021 — each interviewed a storyteller featured in these chapters, learning about them and exploring their nexus of social justice and their respective sport. In the spirit of empathy, students composed these stories as though they were the storytellers, and after multiple drafts and revisions, the chapters you're about to read have been approved by the storytellers since, after all, these stories are theirs and theirs alone.

Therefore, what you're about to read is a very real and powerful narrative — and very personal. The storytellers' views and opinions are their own and not necessarily the same as the students' or ours or the institutions acknowledged in another section of this book. Some chapters contain strong language and/or graphic anecdotes meant not to shock or exploit but instead to bolster readers' knowledge, understanding, and empathy.

We want to thank you — the reader — in advance for taking the time to engage with these stories. Some chapters will inspire hope in you and maybe even prompt change or action. Some will undoubtedly anger you. Some might seem to end abruptly and without a satisfying conclusion, and that's simply because most of these lived experiences are not yet complete. As we've learned throughout this book project, social-justice issues in sports are complex and emotional, and it can be hard to tell it like it is. But at the end of the day, we ask that you do what the student writers did: listen.

Finally, we want to extend our sincere gratitude to our storytellers. You embraced your own vulnerability, entrusting your story with somebody else and working with them to make sure it's accurate and compelling for all who read and learn from it. This book wouldn't exist without you.

* Editor's Note: In general, The Facing Project tries to adhere to American Psychological Association Style protocols for its content. However, for this book, we also integrated the Associated Press' stylistic protocol to capitalize Black whenever used in reference to race or race relations in these chapters.

FOREWORD

Robby General, Sports Reporter & Columnist
The Star Press—USA TODAY Network

Following the Los Angeles Lakers' regular season victory over the Portland Trail Blazers on Feb. 26, 2021, LeBron James sat ready to address the media during a postgame video press conference.

During the presser, a question changed the direction of the interview entirely. Instead of talking about James' double-double, which helped snap the Lakers' four-game losing streak, he addressed another issue when asked about the comments AC Milan striker Zlatan Ibrahimovic made toward him.

Ibrahimovic, without using the exact words, told James to "stick to sports."

"Do what you're good at," Ibrahimovic said in an interview. "... I play football because I'm the best at playing football. I'm no politician. If I'd been a politician, I would be doing politics. This is the first mistake famous people do when they become famous and come into a certain status. For me, it is better to avoid certain topics and do what you're best at doing because otherwise it doesn't look good."

James wasn't surprised by Ibrahimovic's comments. He's heard it all before. Without hesitation, James looked into the camera and said:

"At the end of the day, I would never shut up about things that (are) wrong. I preach about my people, and I preach about equality, social injustice, racism, systematic voter suppression, things that go in our community because I was a part of my community at one point and (have) seen the things that (were) going on."

James' serious demeanor took a turn when he thought back to Ibrahimovic's interview from three years earlier — when the world-renowned soccer star said "there is undercover racism." Ibramimovic, then referring to the less-than-preferential treatment he receives from the Swedish media, "This exists; I am 100-percent sure."

To be fair to Ibrahimovic, James *has* stuck to what he's good at.

On top of being one of the greatest basketball players the world has ever seen, James is also a leading voice for social injustice in America. He has donated millions of dollars to schools, continued to speak out on political and social issues, helped form the "More Than a Vote" group, which was created amid the Black Lives Matter protests following the murders of George Floyd and Breonna Taylor, and so much more.

See, this wasn't the first time the Lakers' small forward, one of the most decorated American athletes of all time, was told to stick to basketball — there was the time in 2018 when Fox News host Laura Ingraham told him to "Keep the political comments to yourselves ... shut up and dribble" — and it probably won't be the last.

It would be easy for James to stick to sports. After all, Michael Jordan stayed out of any political discourse throughout his entire career. Jordan even doubled-down on one his most famous quotes —"Republicans buy sneakers too" — during ESPN's "The Last Dance" documentary, which aired in early 2020. Jordan has admitted that he never saw himself as an activist. He also competed at a time when American athletes largely weren't ready to delve into issues outside of their respective sports.

Throughout history, there have been others who were.

There was tennis star Arthur Ashe who, years before Jordan built a dynasty with the Chicago Bulls, spent the final years of his life opposing the South African apartheid and its mistreatment of Haitian refugees among other causes. Ashe's own story is more complicated than that. He grew up in Richmond, Virginia, in the 1950s. Richmond is a city where whites-only signs were then commonplace, and Ashe played tennis, which was then almost exclusively a white-man's game.

Ashe didn't necessarily want to be an activist. During his competitive days, he largely wasn't. But even as he was coping with AIDS following a blood transfusion after a surgery, Ashe admitted in his memoir "Days of Grace" that his inevitable death wasn't the biggest burden he had faced.

"Race is for me a more onerous burden than AIDS," Ashe wrote. "My disease is the result of biological factors over which we, thus far, have had no control. Racism, however, is entirely made by people, and therefore, it hurts and inconveniences infinitely more."

Fighting for racial equality — in sport and society — has been one of the biggest uphill battles American athletes have had to face.

From America's first Black heavyweight boxing champion Jack Johnson to the four Olympic gold medals Jesse Owens won over Adolf Hitler's "superior" Aryan race to Jackie Robinson capturing America's attention during his debut with the Brooklyn Dodgers to Colin Kaepernick peacefully protesting police brutality by kneeling during the national anthem of a preseason football game, there have been dozens of athletes who, over the past century or so, have fought racial inequalities in their sports and in society.

And every time a Black athlete has made a statement, America has showed its true colors.

Every time Jack Johnson knocked out another white challenger, white sportswriters grew increasingly frustrated having to write about the Black heavyweight champion and scrambled to find another worthy challenger. Tommie Smith and John Carlos were vastly criticized for their actions during one of the most tumultuous years in American history, one that saw the assassinations of Dr. Martin Luther King Jr. and Robert F. Kennedy along with the Chicago police beating protestors during the 1968 Democratic National Convention. Decades later, Kaepernick was chastised for his actions, blackballed by the NFL (though team executives won't admit it), and the opinions people have of the former professional quarterback seem split down the middle.

But each time an athlete has made a stand, and each time the American public has rebelled against them, progress has been made.

The world we live in does not grant equal opportunity for everyone. People are judged and punished due to circumstances largely outside of their control. The inequalities surrounding race, sex, sexual orientation, opportunity, and more have existed for as long as humans have existed.

And the color of someone's skin is not the only inequality athletes in American history have stood up for.

Boxing legend Muhammad Ali cited his Muslim faith as a reason for refusing to join the draft in the Vietnam War. He lost his belt and three years of his prime fighting career while fighting for his beliefs.

Inspired by the events of 9/11, Pat Tillman left behind his $3.6-million NFL contract to sign up for the United States Army.

For nearly a decade, Venus Williams fought the tennis world at Wimbledon to make the prize money for both men and women equal. Years before that, in 1967, Kathrine Switzer broke the gender barrier at the Boston Marathon by both running and finishing what was then a men's-only race — and had been since its inception in 1897.

Tatyanna McFadden, a 17-time Paralympic medalist in wheelchair racing, was told she couldn't compete alongside her able-bodied peers. As a result, McFadden sued the state of Maryland and won, which, in 2008, led to Maryland requiring schools to provide equal opportunities for students with disabilities to participate in physical-education programs and compete on athletic teams. In 2013, those state-wide standards became a national mandate.

In 2014, Michael Sam came out as the first openly gay football player a year before the U.S. Supreme Court ruled that same-sex couples are allowed to marry regardless of where they live. Since then, Sam has been vocally fighting for LGBTQ+ rights and suicide prevention.

Fern "Peachy" Kellmeyer and Elaine Gavigan began a lawsuit in the 1970s that fought to allow females to earn college athletic scholarships and led to the enaction of Title IX, which prohibits sex-based discrimination in any school or education program that receives federal money. During that same time, Billie Jean King demanded equality in tennis and beat "male chauvinist pig" Bobby Riggs in the Battles of the Sexes match. In 1973, she forced the U.S. Open to provide the same winnings to both men and women.

Just this past year, Simone Biles, one of the most decorated gymnasts of all time, withdrew from the Summer Olympics in Tokyo — the biggest stage of the sport — because of a mental-health issue. Biles' decision created a domino effect of athletes who came out to discuss the mental-health battles they've faced.

It would have been easy for these athletes — then and now — to stick to their sports, smile, take their checks, and hide from the problems they face every day. After all, against the odds, they've made it. But these athletes have chosen to stand for something more. They realized they had a voice and a platform to make a difference bigger than winning a game, medal, or world championship.

Throughout our world's history, it has been hard enough for anyone other than a white male to become a prominent figure in the sports world let alone fight for social-justice issues while also trying to appeal to a society that — to this day — remains split on so many issues. Even as our society has progressed, it has made sense why athletes were able to or even interested in taking a stand.

With the rise of technology and social media, more athletes have been finding their voices. They know the social-justice issues that society faces because they've seen them. They've lived them. And they've realized that they can make a difference. These athlete advocates and activists aren't asking for preferential treatment or that everyone be like them. They never have been. They're just fighting for an equal playing field for all.

And who better to level the playing field than athletes?

Sports and society have been intertwined throughout our history. From influencing fashion, pop culture, and politics, athletes are in a unique situation to be a catalyst for change in society.

Over the past decade, we've seen a resurgence in athletic advocacy and activism. And it's not just coming from the professionals anymore.

Those names — Ali, James, Tillman, Williams, Biles — are just the ones you've heard of. There are more and more athletes finding their voices and fighting for the social-justice issues that they believe in.

There's Jessie Bates III who, growing up without a father, realized how important it was for young kids to have someone to teach them lessons that a father would. There's Trey Moses who lost his best friend to suicide and has since dedicated his life to help people with mental-health issues to accept, talk about, and live with those issues. There's CJ Allard who never thought he'd be an advocate for international, collegiate student-athletes but quickly realized how hard their lives are moving while thousands of miles from their homes. There's Dan Leventhal who, as a white man coaching predominantly Black lacrosse athletes in the Bronx, realized how important it is to listen to the stories and lives of those you simply cannot understand.

The sports these athletes and coaches play and what they — including all the storytellers in this book — fight for might be different, but their goals are essentially the same.

The stories of the athletes, coaches, mentors, and sports-media professionals you are about to read are fighting for causes they are passionate about. They're fighting to give a voice to those who may not have one, highlighting issues that those of privilege might not understand and holding leaders accountable for their actions.

The fight for social justice has been happening well before a football player "disrespected the flag" or a basketball player was told to "shut up and dribble."

Maybe one day student-athletes won't have to protest for racial and gender equality within their academic institutions. Maybe one day everybody might have the resources they need to succeed. Maybe one day people will be able to listen to each other work with and for those who need it most.

Maybe one day a professional athlete like LeBron James will be able to sit in a postgame press conference with nothing else to worry about than how his team played that night.

Maybe one day social justice will truly exist.

Today is not that day. And so tomorrow, they will get up and continue fighting until that day comes.

Love It Or Hate It — You're Aware Of It

The Polarization of Colin Kaepernick

by **Andrew Kahle**

When Colin Kaepernick sat on the bench as the national anthem played before an Aug. 26, 2016, game against the Green Bay Packers, it's doubtful he thought it would receive so much attention. Besides, it wasn't the first time he had sat during the national anthem. It was just the first time the media took notice — just hours before it became a national talking point.

Before the day ended, Kaepernick was the talk of the sports world. Many took to social media, some tweeting that Kaepernick's actions were "un-American" (Biderman, 2016) and others shrugging him off as a millionaire with no right to complain (Desmond-Harris, 2016). During the San Francisco 49ers' next game, he knelt rather than sat throughout the national anthem, and he was joined in protest by teammate Eric Reid (who would kneel alongside Kaepernick throughout the season). Within the next week, the U.S. president was commenting on his actions, and many players joined Kaepernick in kneeling during the national anthem on the first Sunday of the 2016 season.

Nearly two years after Kaepernick's pregame protests were first noticed by the media, the NFL announced a rule that stated that NFL players would be fined for sitting or kneeling during the national anthem, and Kaepernick hadn't played since December of 2016.

"And five years later, you're still asking me about it," said columnist Gregg Doyel of *The Indianapolis Star*. "I think it (Kaepernick's decision to kneel) was brilliant; there's no better way to raise awareness. People say, 'Go do it somewhere else.' (But) nobody would care if he'd done that anywhere else. We are a star-struck culture, and you're on the biggest sports stage. Who better to inform and raise awareness on these issues other than sports stars?"

Even though players like Eric Reid and Torrey Smith agreed with Kaepernick's actions, some 49ers players questioned Kaepernick's decision to kneel when it was first noticed by the media. Some said there was a "better way" to go about it, while others called it a distraction to the team or questioned if it was a swipe at military servicemen and servicewomen (NFL, 2016).

"Honestly, I don't think there was any approach that would have been more pragmatic. People in sports have always brought social justice and awareness to sports," said Sarah Mitchell, editor of Morehead State University's (Kentucky) *Trail Blazer*. "People have protested quietly; some have taken that extra step. Kaepernick wasn't aggressive or off-putting or anti-American, but he wanted to bring attention to something. He took that extra step. What better way to do that — to bring awareness — than during a game that has thousands of viewers? People being so buzzed about it proves that he did something significant. Whether you want to perceive it as a positive or a negative, what he did caught your eye and got your attention; it made an impact. And that impact has caused a ripple effect through other sports too. He threw himself into the limelight and got Americans' attention. People can say he's being disrespectful or he's taking a stand, but either way, you're aware of it. He did his part by bringing your attention to these issues and why they're so critically important."

Over half a decade later (but maybe what feels like a full decade later), there is still no shortage of awareness when it comes to the movement that Kaepernick sparked. There is still no shortage of controversy surrounding the subject either. If anything, Kaepernick was proven to be as polarizing a figure as he'd ever been when he became the face of an advertisement campaign for Nike in September

2018. As was the case when the media first took notice of him sitting on the bench during the national anthem, many applauded him. Many also burnt his jersey and swore off Nike, much as they had the NFL.

"I'm a huge supporter of BLM and Kaepernick's protests, but it's been a fart in the wind as far as changing anyone's mind goes," said columnist Gregg Doyel. "Mike Pence left that Colts game in 2017; fans burned his (Kaepernick's) jersey; NFL ratings and crowds are both down. Both sides just dug their heels in deeper."

At times, with so much pushback to Kaepernick's efforts to bring awareness to racial inequalities, it can seem as if nothing has changed. Even some NFL players, such as former Dallas Cowboys receiver Dez Bryant, have respectfully criticized Kaepernick's movement. Bryant, speaking on the "I Am Athlete" podcast, questioned whether or not there was a call to action or any legitimate change brought on by his protest (Lanier, 2021). Yet the fact that Kaepernick's actions are still so polarizing — half a decade later — still brings attention and awareness to racial inequalities whether one agrees with his methods or not. The ripples of Kaepernick's protests can still be seen in 2021 where the NFL allows social-justice messaging on players' helmets and includes social-justice messaging on the field itself. His protests expanded into other sports' leagues with players from the NBA, WNBA, and MLB all showing their support and joining Kaepernick in kneeling during the national anthem. Even years later, some high school and collegiate athletes (such as a portion of Virginia Tech's volleyball team or the Ole Miss men's basketball team) have joined the protests, expressing their rights and their demands for progress on racial inequalities.

"We've helped broadcast a few games with ESPN, and even in those few games, you'll see a few athletes taking a knee during the anthem," said Taylor Johnson, sports photographer and photo editor for Morehead State University's (Kentucky) *Trail Blazer*. "I've seen it at football and basketball games; I even saw it at a softball game. It may not be the case everywhere, but what's great is you see these athletes making their stance known, and in every instance I've seen, they've got teammates there kneeling with and supporting them."

Judging the impacts of Kaepernick's protests as a whole is difficult to do — even five years later. It can also be difficult for some to comprehend what sacrifices were made by Kaepernick in kneeling during the anthem.

"It's a bold move. Someone who was doing what he loved, making millions of dollars," said Nate Fields, prep sports assistant for *The Cincinnati Enquirer*. "Being able to give that up to stand for what you believe in says a lot of him as a person, and he just went out there, (and) he spoke his mind; he demonstrated what so many people were thinking. It takes a lot of guts. It's not easy to give something up that you worked toward your whole life."

With widespread support from other athletes, fans, politicians, and some of the sports leagues themselves, the movement seems as alive in 2021 as when NFL players joined Kaepernick in protest on the first Sunday of the 2016 season. Kaepernick's decision has had an effect on more than just the playing field. He's inspired other players to make an impact: be it by giving a voice to their beliefs or making an impact in their communities.

"You see it now with players like Malcolm Brogdon from the (Indiana) Pacers — players getting out in the community where they can stand behind their cause and take some action," said Nate Fields of *The Cincinnati Enquirer*. "I feel there have been more open policies, especially watching the NBA or WNBA, where players have done different things from kneeling to walking off the court to protest games. And it seems now that in those cases, the Leagues have had their back."

It's true: Some may not believe Kaepernick's actions were effective, or they may think that he should have attempted to communicate his message somewhere else. Others, however, feel as if he's had a historic impact on the landscape of sports.

"I think he's (Kaepernick's) going to be held up there with Jackie Robinson and Muhammad Ali," said columnist Gregg Doyel of *The Indianapolis Star*. "They changed the world, and he's certainly helped to do the same."

RESOURCES

Biderman, C. (2016, October 16). *Colin Kaepernick has strong response to being called 'un-American'.* USA Today. Retrieved November 16, 2021, from https://ninerswire.usatoday.com/2016/10/16/colin-kaepernick-has-strong-response-to-being-called-un-american/.

Desmond-Harris, J. (2016, August 27). *If you think millionaire athlete Colin Kaepernick is too rich to protest, you don't understand activism.* Vox. Retrieved November 18, 2021, from https://www.vox.com/2016/8/27/12673388/kaepernick-49ers-race-racism-protest-police.

Lanier, J. (2021, September 29). *Dez Bryant criticizes Colin Kaepernick's protest for having 'No Call to Action'.* Outsider. Retrieved November 16, 2021, from https://outsider.com/news/sports/dez-bryant-criticizes-colin-kaepernicks-protest-having-no-call-action/.

Moseley, B. (2020, January 6). *Byrne calls Kaepernick a jerk, suggests he is un-American.* Alabama Political Reporter. Retrieved November 22, 2021, from https://www.alreporter.com/2020/01/06/byrne-calls-kaepernick-a-jerk-suggests-he-is-un-american/.

NFL. (2016, August 28). *Colin Kaepernick: I'll continue to sit during national anthem.* NFL.com. Retrieved November 28, 2021, from https://www.nfl.com/news/colin-kaepernick-i-ll-continue-to-sit-during-national-anthem-0ap3000000691874.

CHAPTER 1: MOMMA'S BOY

JESSIE BATES III'S STORY AS TOLD TO MITCHELL CARTER

Key Words: Male, Pro-Football, Athlete, Race, Indiana/Ohio

The car had hit a snowbank and stopped in its tracks. A half mile away from the site of the shooting, Anderson Retic and Joshua Cole Cooper lay slumped in their seats — dead; Jaylin Rice was in critical condition. These three young Black men were gunned down after an argument with Joseph Bossard, a white man inside of a gas station in my hometown of Fort Wayne, Indiana. Empty bullet casings littered the gas station parking lot, and blood spattered the inside of the car that the boys were driving to escape. I don't live in Fort Wayne anymore, but my mom does, and so do my siblings and many of my close friends.

That shooting broke my heart; those young Black men could have easily been my friends and me. I believe that it was a hate crime, and that's not the Fort Wayne that I know.

Before I was a standout safety for the Wake Forest Demon Deacons football team or an All-Pro safety for the Cincinnati Bengals, it was just me, my mom, and my siblings trying to get by in my hometown of Fort Wayne. While I had no father figure in the home growing up, I had

1

mentors and people close to me who were responsible for leading me on the right path. Not just in the football sense but in life too.

Football is a game of inches. It's violent, but it's also strategic. Football, basketball, and baseball were all the sports that my mom put me into when I was a kid. I made a lot of friends and found that I excelled at all of those sports, but it was pretty apparent that football was where I had the best chance for a future. I was a young man growing up in a single-parent household, and the opportunity to continue my football career in college with a scholarship was one that I couldn't wait to pursue. I wasn't aware of just how many doors would be opened for me through football, and for that, I owe football a lot. However, I don't think it would have all been possible if I hadn't also played basketball and baseball. Those two sports allowed me to train in other ways, honing other skills that are important in football but not necessarily as focused on. Not only that, but I also got to compete in some capacity all year, and I think that constant competitiveness in my life allowed me to stay hungry, always working toward my next goal.

Bowling, on the other hand, isn't quite as violent as football, but secretly, I've grown to love it too. One of my close friends growing up, Trevor Wilson, better known as Trimmer Trev, is not only my barber but also a pretty proficient bowler. For my birthday, he got me my first pair of bowling shoes. I ended up buying my own ball not long after, and he won't admit it, but sometimes I'll beat him. If you're going to be good at one sport, might as well be good at them all.

Social justice isn't as cut and dry as football or bowling. You can't watch tape and scout social justice, and you don't need to get your ankles taped up before you take on social justice. Things that have been making headlines in our country — police brutality, racism, equality issues — those have been going on for years and years. It's just now coming up on a lot of people's radars, though, and while there is change being made, and I think that's great, I feel that everything that has happened boils down to human rights.

Speaking on what just happened in Fort Wayne. Those three boys were gunned down in their hometown, and I really do believe that if they were white, we wouldn't have seen them on the news; besides an argument, nothing would have happened. I believe those young men were gunned down by a white man because they were Black. It's a hate crime, simple as that. If we can't eliminate things like that in our society, how much progress are we really making?

2

When it comes to speaking out on social justice, there are so many things that are important to me. I know that I'm not alone in my thoughts about racial injustice, police brutality, and human rights, but I'll be the first to admit that I probably haven't been as outspoken as I would have liked to be.

I feel like this generation is all about the hype, and it's cool to get behind what issues are hot in the moment. I think it's more important to be educated on a subject before speaking on it. First, educate yourself and then educate your family and friends. That's where you're really going to be making a difference. A lot of my focus has gone toward educating myself and my family and less toward speaking out publicly about issues, but I'm looking to change that as I grow and mature as a person and an athlete.

When I was in high school, I was a part of AWP, Athletes With Purpose. Their mission was to develop not only the body of young athletes but also the mind. We worked hard, competing day in and day out in drills, workouts, and sometimes 7-on-7 competitions. At the same time, though, all who were a part of AWP were taught lessons about how to be better men and not just better athletes.

I strive to be just that — an athlete with purpose.

I think we have a major problem as a society where we ostracize athletes who utilize their platforms to speak up on issues that are important to them. How can you tell somebody who's a person just like you are to just "shut up and dribble?" We hurt too; we have opinions and fears just like the rest of you. That's where I feel like AWP really helped me grow not only as a person but also as a player. You can't fix everything that's wrong with the world, but if you have the courage and passion to stand up and speak on an issue that's important to you, you can at least make a start.

Growing up without a father figure in the home, I sought the help and guidance of Michael V. Ledo, the CEO of AWP and now the CEO of RISE Sports Advisors. He was always pushing me. He saw the potential in me, but he also constantly reminded me that all of the potential in the world means nothing if you don't continue to apply yourself every single day, especially when it comes to educating yourself. He was always in touch with me throughout college, and he's still educating me to this day. He's an integral part of my management

3

team now in the NFL, and he along with some others are the ones who ensure that I have both a financial and physical plan for myself on and off of the field.

One of the big problems about growing up with only your mom in the home is just the lack of education about things that fathers talk about with their sons.

I don't think that there's enough we can do to push education with the younger generation, especially those kids who are growing up just like I did. I've been in the National Football League a few years now, and I decided that the best way to utilize my resources and my drive to give back to the community was to start the JB3 Single Mother's Initiative as well as creating some JB3 Summits in my home town of Fort Wayne.

Through my Single Mother's Initiative, I've gotten to partner with the Boys and Girls Club in Cincinnati and bring some kids and their mothers to a Bengals game followed by dinner with me. It'd be really easy for me to just throw some money at a program or charity and call it good, but I think there's merit in letting the kids see your face, talk with you, and have an experience that they'll never forget. Sitting down with those kids and their moms, seeing them all smile, laugh, and enjoy themselves is why I do it. I want those kids to see somebody who grew up not so different from them and made it. I'm not exactly sure where it'll go from here, but I love where it's headed.

I tried to apply the same principles with my JB3 Summits. Unfortunately, due to COVID-19, we didn't get to have one this year, but the plan was to have a bunch of guest speakers come in with me and partner with the Fort Wayne community schools and just talk with them. There were so many things that I had no idea about growing up: stocks and bonds, personal finance, and even sex. It's so important to me to give these kids the opportunity to be educated on subjects at a young age that I wasn't able to learn until I was older — some of it not until I was out of college.

I won't pretend to act like I'm a father figure to these kids, but maybe I can offer some lessons that a father should.

The same thing applies to the JB3 Summits as does my Single Mother's Initiative: There's power in these kids getting to see me and interact with me. I was in a lot of their shoes not too long ago, and I

4

think just knowing that I have the opportunity and the power to make a difference is what gets me the most excited.

Football has opened up doors and opportunities for me that I never would have thought possible. I didn't come from money, and there are people just like me who haven't gotten and may never get the opportunities I have. I'm not blind to the fact that I've been incredibly blessed, and I feel it's my opportunity to continue providing for my family and educating not only myself but those close to me. Our country has been around for a long time, and the only way that we're going to continue moving forward and battling injustices is for us all to take a step back and understand what's really at hand and what we can do to change it.

Chapter 2: Internal And External

Brian Richardson Jr.'s Story As Told to Tahj Reeves

Key Words: Male, Pro-Football, DEI Director, Race, Indiana

"Why do you sit in front of the class?"

"How many grills do you have?"

"Do you smoke crack?"

These were just some questions asked of me at my predominantly white institution I attended as an undergrad, but they're something I have remembered. The majority of the comments weren't hurtful, but they didn't know any better. They had never been around anyone who wasn't white — a minority. Their community was everyone who looked similar to them, so when a change happened, they were curious. I didn't take the comments to heart, but I wanted to use my personal experiences to help them better understand minorities, so the next time they would meet someone who was different than them, comments like those wouldn't be made again.

My name is Brian Richardson Jr., and I am the director of diversity, equity, and inclusion for the Indianapolis Colts.

My role came into play in December 2020, so my role is still fairly new. The Indianapolis Colts is now a community I am a part of, but when I say community, what do I mean by that?

When I talk about the Colts, there are two forms of community: internal and external. The internal community is the employees, players, staff, and anybody who works for the Colts organization. And the opposite goes for the external community, so this would be the greater Indianapolis area, its residents, and the Colts' fanbase.

In our internal community, we do many things for diversity, equity, and inclusion. We set a plan that has four core functional areas: ongoing educational opportunities, which are activities such as panels, workshops, and discussions, but also passive elements such as monthly email newsletters that feature historical context, facts and figures, upcoming programs, and a list of local organizations and businesses that are owned and operated by diverse communities. The other three core functional areas include a focus on community engagement and relations, recruitment and retention, and supplier diversity.

Currently, we are recognizing each heritage month. For example, during Hispanic heritage month, we brought in faculty members of Latinx descent from Earlham College, IUPUI, a local government official, and a representative from Anthem Blue Cross Blue Shield. We had them on a Zoom call (to follow COVID-19 protocols) to speak with our internal community about how to create inclusive spaces for Latinx individuals, really to explain who is included in the "Latinx" term, discuss how to overcome common stereotypes, and tips on how to be an ally to the community in and outside of the workplace.

Regarding the second area, community engagement and relations, we are currently highlighting how we can work together with the external community to build genuine relationships with members of different communities.

When I highlight local organizations that are doing work within their community, I am building those relationships with leaders and community members. It is about how we, the Colts, can come alongside them and be good stewards and partners in the work. We know that by speaking up and supporting various causes, our platform

7

allows us to bring more awareness to the topics and causes the organization is about. Connecting with the community also grants me access to local leaders who are able to speak at our educational panels, internally, for our employees. These opportunities have provided a platform for local leaders to then share their work, knowledge, and expertise.

The third area is recruitment and retention. This spans from our interns to our full-time positions. We are establishing an access point for people to be aware of job postings and how to get in the sports field.

For instance, I have partnered with historically Black colleges/universities and Hispanic-serving institutions, and I'm currently planning on establishing partnerships with all-women colleges and tribal colleges as part of our strategic approach.

Recently, the White House Initiative launched its first-ever HBCU career fair, and I received over 114 résumés. I got to talk to students about when the Colts have internships and when job opportunities appear. These conversations are centered around promoting opportunities within sports, teaching the students what it looks like to work in sports, how to find jobs, and things you should put into your résumé. My goal is to give these students an education when applying for jobs: what they should expect, what dates they should be aware of, and what places to go to find jobs. My instruction goes beyond sports jobs and applies to any jobs they will be applying for.

The fourth area is supplier diversity. This programming is still currently in the process. But what we as an organization plan to do is to review contracts of existing partners to ask questions internally like: who are we hiring, how diverse is our organization, what businesses are we supporting (are they Black-owned, woman-owned, minority-owned)? For us to thoroughly understand supplier diversity, we are currently analyzing what is already in place. We are doing some internal assessments to see what can change and where are we currently making strides.

Internal and external community go hand-in-hand — but there are differences.

External community is also something we value at the Colts' organization. Recently, we have been able to do some work outside the office.

For example, we showed solidarity with the LGBTQ+ community for Pride Month. We let the community know they have our full support through our social media platforms, serving as a sponsor to LGBTQ+ organizations and having personal videos of solidarity featured in the Indy Pride Month Annual Festival, which was held online in 2020 due to COVID-19. Not only this but things such as supporting minority-owned businesses and letting the public know about important issues.

The future is always bright, so we are looking at how to keep the external and internal communities strong.

My position with the team is still new, but we strive to continue navigating and building on the four functional areas. We have committed to continue to support minority-owned businesses, support social-justice organizations, and make great connections with the external community. I am excited to see what happens in the future because this is only the beginning.

CHAPTER 3: MORE THAN A QUOTA

TAYLOR TANNEBAUM'S STORY AS TOLD TO BRYCE WHARTON

Key Words: Female, Pro-All Sports, Reporter/Anchor, Gender Equality, Indiana/Florida/Alabama

Strength. Knowledgeable. Informative.

Those are just a few things that women in the sports industry must have or be. Do not give people a reason to doubt you; they will find any reason to. This is earned and not given. I am in the position I am in for a reason. We deserve to be here.

That is the vibe you get from the all the female athletes, coaches, and people in the marketing positions and beyond. We have all worked to get here, and we are proud of that. But we need more women in the sports industry. Just because we are women does not mean we can't be educated on sports or even have a passion for it.

My childhood was surrounded by sports. I grew up going to watch sports because my family had season tickets to most Florida teams. I grew up playing sports. I played soccer and flag football in high school because I went to a school with Title IX sports. My dad owned memorabilia stores, so every Saturday, there would be autograph sessions from collegiate athletes to professional athletes. I have albums and albums with autographs — from people I do not even know!

I was always exposed to it. I knew early in high school that I wanted to get into sports media.

I like the direction we are going by including women more in sports. I feel like it's growing at least on the TV side. When I moved to Alabama in 2013, I was the first female sports anchor in all of Dothan. Here at WTHR in Indianapolis, I am the first female sports anchor, but there have been women in this market. I used to walk into a locker room with 30 reporters and be the only female. Now, I could see five female sports reporters out of 30. So I think it is moving in the right direction, but I think we still have ways to go.

Do not just do it once — keep making those hires. Yes, she can be the first, but she cannot be the last. Let's do it because they deserve it.

Most sports departments in the country have one female, but I hope that changes. There is still a huge ratio disparity, and I would say that comes from the print side. We need to respect women more as writers. People are going to want to think what they want to think at the end of the day, but I think that you just have to believe in yourself. If you know you can do it, do it!

The best way to empower other women is to encourage them. Encourage them to be themselves; encourage them to try new things.

Supporting each other is key. If someone is hating on you for liking sports, it means they are uncomfortable in their own skin. There are many men who would look at that and say, "That is really awesome." Just because you know something another woman might not does not make you bad or different; instead, it just makes you more knowledgeable. There is nothing wrong with that. If someone thinks that is strange, I think that is a personal problem. If sports is your thing, own it.

Everyone loves something different, so be confident in what you love. One thing I say is do not compare yourself to other people or to other people's journey. Everyone has their own journey.

There is not a single person in this industry who has had the same journey. Not the way it works. Your opportunity will come. This is not the typical, moving-up-in-the-rankings job. You have to find opportunities upon opportunities, and that may take you to different cities and areas. Just do your job, and the best thing to do in this business is to make connections.

So grind until you cannot grind anymore. Your time will come.

True, this industry can be discouraging. Women can be very competitive. You have to realize there is room for everybody. You can lift up other women. Compliment them on their work. You can mentor other women. When they ask for advice, take the time and give it. Even if they don't come to you, reach out. If positions open, but you're above that position already, push for another woman to fill that position. Say, "I have a woman who would be great for you!"

Shining a light on each other is important. When something is significant, we do a good job of showcasing it. Which is good; it shows other women who look like her that they can do it too.

For me, when I was in high school and watching TV, Erin Andrews started to pop up on the scene. They would showcase her a lot on social media, and she was the younger sideline College Gameday reporter. She was a really cool woman just talking sports with the guys, and that's what I aspired to do. She was there for those big moments.

I have been fortunate to be part of great sports moments too. For instance, I have been to four NCAA football championships. I covered Alabama and Auburn football; I was there when Chris Davis returned the missed field goal to send Auburn to the National Championship in 2013. Where they played my alma mater, Florida State, and I had just graduated.

I was able to go to the final Rose Bowl in Pasadena that was in the Bowl Championship Series (BCS) era. I have been able to cover the Indianapolis 500 — so cool! A bucket-list item for any sports fan. Being able to be inside of Hinkle Fieldhouse, Mackey Arena, and Assembly Hall. Places that have a vibe where it just does not compare.

For football, Auburn vs. Alabama is the big deal, but for basketball, it is IU vs. Purdue. Since moving to Indiana, I have been able to be a part of that rivalry, and nothing beats the atmosphere of Mackey

Arena when it is packed. It is just unbelievable! Just being in those atmospheres has allowed me to see some incredible things and meet some incredible people.

I have also been fortunate to work with great male colleagues and athletes on my journey. When I am in the locker rooms, they are cordial. They haven't said inappropriate things while I am in there. I have been blessed to work with lots of male colleagues. I am grateful for the men I have encountered in this career. They have only made me better, supported me, and given me opportunities. Even with those great moments and male co-workers, you will have the people who will hoot and holler, "You're hot," or "You're pretty," whereas my male counterparts will not have that kind of talk happening to him while he is trying to work.

People do not know that still happens, but I think they should know.

I have had that encounter recently — just last year actually. It doesn't happen a lot, but it does happen.

A man attending a sporting event was being creepy and just completely inappropriate. I had never met the man. He was not even from Indianapolis. He was just traveling for the sport I was covering. And he got way too close to me and whispered in my ear. He made a comment of what I was wearing and how it looked on me. Something that even if it is a compliment ... it was something you just should not say to a woman.

Encounters like that take away from your job. It makes you feel like someone is watching you, studying you, and it makes it harder to work.

When you are in a moment and something happens to you, it's hard to react right away. In that particular moment, I just wanted to run and tell somebody what happened. It made my job really hard to do, but you just have to roll with the punches. Let them know it is not allowed, and let your supervisor know what is going on. It sucks in the moment, but you have to remember: You can only control what you do.

I did the rest of my job that day. I went home; I decompressed; I talked to my bosses and got it off my chest, and that's all you can really do.

It is a stressful job, but I like the stress of it. I am a bit of a thrill seeker, and it is satisfying to know you accomplish something every day. I wake up happy to go to work, and that is how I know I still want to do this.

My message for other women trying to achieve more in this industry: Do not give up. Stay the course.

Sports connect people in a way that nothing else can. Talking to other women in sports, I have learned that we are resilient. We are willing to take on the challenge of proving people wrong. There are good women out there. We are very knowledgeable. We do want to learn. And we are grinders.

Chapter 4: Racing Forward

Logan Ray's Story as Told to Ali Spires

Key Words: Male, Pro-NASCAR, Pit Crew, Race, Indiana

Sweat covers my face. I can feel it burning my eyes and taste the saltiness on my lips. I can't use my hands to wipe it off or I risk staining my face with the thin layer of black that covers them. Oil, tread from tires ... who the hell knows. I can feel the sun beating down, and heat radiates up off the black pavement under my feet. The engines are roaring next to me, begging for me to start the race.

I'm yelling, "Run!" as loud as I can over the cars, and the lead singer of Rascal Flatts begins sprinting toward me. As if the days are not stressful enough, everyone is waiting on me to get the celebrity guest into the car to start the first lap of the race. He's not going to make it. Please just get here in time. I'm throwing him into the pace car as 30 IndyCars begin charging our direction. I barely make it out of the way when I feel the air rush over me as they roar past.

There's nothing like a race day.

But there's been a lack of representation from the very beginning. In the racing industry, "minority" pretty much means anyone who isn't a

15

straight, white guy. That applies to the racers, teams, owners, sponsors, and even to the fan base. The most obvious lack of representation we see in IndyCar comes from a lack of women and the Black community.

I blame the history of the sport. For too long, the racing industry has been associated with white men, cold beer, and loud cars. Don't get me wrong: It's all those things, but it could be so much more if inclusion was more of a priority.

I've worked in Speedway, Indiana, "The race capital of the world," for a little over a year now. Within that short time, I've been head of EMI Graphix, the main graphics company for Speedway Indiana and IndyCar. I've traveled to numerous tracks and races across the country and have experienced the unique environment of racing. There's an intensity that can't even really be described. It's an aggressive sport that provokes passion from all those who work in the industry not to mention the fans. If racing is anything, it's loud. Besides just the engines, it's a bunch of men yelling at each other. Whether it's men in the stands screaming for their favorite drivers or all of us working in the pits and yelling at one another to hurry up and get our shit done in time. It's a lot.

I think this type of atmosphere isn't always the most welcoming in general, but I think it's especially uninviting for women. I think the intensity surrounding the sport has often been a deterrent for women to get involved. It's also been a common excuse that men have used to justify why women don't belong in certain aspects of the sport. Most women you see in the industry are going to be working behind a desk, in PR, or advertising for some sponsor and are there solely based on their looks.

Now, I'm sure a significant amount of reasoning for the lack of women on the track itself is due to certain criteria of the jobs available and a lack of women interested in them. Many jobs in racing are physically demanding, dirty, unglamorous grunt work. However, there are some women working in these positions already, including an all-female race team. So that's not to say that women aren't willing or are unable to do these jobs; they just typically aren't as interested in them or at least aren't being given the same chance at these positions as their male peers.

Honestly, it's a shame that more women aren't involved in the entirety of the racing industry.

Within my whole company, there are two women, and I'll tell you what: They get shit done! We could not function without them, and they are two of the most respected members of our team. One of these women is Shonda Kennedy, and she's the sales and marketing executive assistant. Shonda is responsible for all of our traveling, daily schedules, client relations, and just about anything else important you could think of. She also helps to maintain a healthy work environment. When it's been an intense day at the track and the guys aren't worried about being nice to each other, she steps in and makes sure everyone is doing okay and treated respectfully. Women add a valuable perspective and demographic to the sport of racing, and the more female representation we can get in the industry the better. More representation of all for that matter.

Since its existence, the racing industry has struggled with representation of the Black community. A huge part of this is due to the reputation that the racing industry is the sport of rednecks.

People often assume a sport's inclusiveness based on the majority of the fan base that is associated with it.

In the case of racing, the crowd is often a bunch of white men who are assumed to be southern and racist. This is obviously a serious issue when trying to immerse the Black community into the racing world because why the hell would they want to go somewhere they feel unwelcome or unrepresented?

A large part of the fan base is made of the stereotypical, patriotic, middle-class, white guy. These are men who are drinking beer, watching fast cars, and are there to appreciate the highest level of blue-collar work that one can do. Classism is very apparent in the race industry, and money is often a key factor in the lack of diversity in racing. Most big-time racers are coming from family money — generations of wealth allowing them to participate. Breaking into the race world costs a pretty penny, which limits who is able to successfully venture into the sport. It's unfortunate because I truly think the industry and the fans are ready and excited for diversity on the track and in the stands.

One of the biggest pushes for diversity we're seeing in racing right now is the introduction of the Race for Equality and Change initiative. For example, Force Indy, a Black-owned race team, was created within this initiative and has partnered with Penske to focus on developing diverse talent within the racing world. The main goal is to grow the sport ethnically, educationally, and across genders. We're striving to achieve inclusivity and diversity for the remaining future of racing.

They've done nothing but impress.

Recently, Force Indy celebrated one of the biggest milestones in racing to date. Myles Rowe, 21, became the first Black driver to ever win an IndyCar-sanctioned race. That's fucking awesome! Within the short year the program has been in place, we're already seeing this huge victory for diversity and the racing industry as a whole.

Diversity and inclusion are going to be key to the survival and success of any sport. Admittedly, racing has a lot of catching up to do and a lot of room for improvement in these areas. With that said, though, I think the industry should be excited at how much growth we will experience in the upcoming seasons as diversity is achieved within the sport. I personally am excited for the day that I can see a little girl on her dad's shoulders, or a young Black son holding his dad's hand, point up to the big screen at the track and say, "Hey, that person looks like me. Maybe I could do that!"

We have a long road ahead of us, and I'm ready to start racing forward.

Chapter 5: Why Listening Is So Important

Zach Hughes' Story as Told to Charleston Bowles

Key Words: Male, Pro-Women's Basketball, Digital Marketing Coordinator, Race, Indiana

Racial injustice. A topic that has been glossed over for decades, specifically in the realm of sports.

The days of ignoring it are over. If the dialogue and events that took place in 2020 taught us anything, it proved how passionate our sports figures are on this subject.

Whether you agree with their stances or not, you must acknowledge what they have to say. While it might be hard for some, we must listen to the figures on the front lines to truly understand where they are coming from.

I sat down and listened during the 2020 summer protests, which I consider a pivotal role in my own journey with racial injustice.

As a white guy from central Indiana, I have never experienced racial injustice. It was a very important summer for me to sit back and hear from others whether that be in person or over Zoom calls.

I started to communicate with Indiana Fever players and listened to their honest perspectives on the tragedies of Breonna Taylor and George Floyd. As Black women, our players gravitated toward Taylor's story in particular. They used it as fuel for change. Our players made it clear they're Black women before they're professional athletes.

As soon as they step off the court, they can easily be the next Breonna Taylor.

It's not just a certain fraction or group of players who have these uncomfortable conversations. Every player is involved and deeply invested in advancing the discussion. They all believe it's worth risking their profession to stand up for what they believe in. This is their life.

Thankfully, the WNBA listened.

The League got behind them and made things happen this summer in the bubble at IMG Academy in Bradenton, Florida. This is where the WNBA gathered each team together and isolated them to conduct the rest of their season and playoffs, which were halted by the virus outbreak in March 2020. The players were tested for COVID-19 daily, and they were required to stay within the IMG campus only until their team was eliminated from the playoffs. Before entering the bubble, the League made it clear to the players they were encouraged to use their platforms. Every player had Taylor's name on the back of their jerseys, and the warmup shirts read "Black Lives Matter." The court also contained logos of "Black Lives Matter" on the center-court and baseline logos.

One of the most passionate athletes during the summer was Natalie Achonwa. As a daughter of a white mother and Black father, she brought a unique perspective to the discussion. She focused her message on starting conversations regarding racial injustice within your family because you cannot impact strangers unless you're impacting the ones who love you.

Although Achonwa left for the Minnesota Lynx in the offseason, her leadership and thoughts did not go unnoticed within the Fever organization.

She helped create the "Fever For Change" fund that raised money for local nonprofits that give back to the youth and make Indianapolis a better place. The Fever raised $15,740 for the Dr. Martin Luther King Jr. Center, Indy Urban Acres, Indiana Youth Group, and Women4Change.

The Dr. Martin Luther King Jr. Center provides resources to the families of northern Indianapolis, while Indy Urban Acres helps solve urban health problems by promoting healthy food choices. Indiana Youth Group helps 12-20-year-olds who identify as a part of the LGBTQ+ community find their path in life. Lastly, Women4Change is an organization that encourages its members to practice acts of equality and inclusion in the Indianapolis area.

There has been a lot of internal discussion within the Fever management on how we can actually start making a lasting impact beyond marching. We just launched the "Athletes To Advocates" initiative, which partners with IUPUI's School of Philanthropy. For the next five weeks, a handful of our players and a few life coaches will be taking courses on how to channel their energy and direct their focus to specific philanthropic efforts as opposed to just tweeting about it. Tamika Catchings, who spent 15 years playing for the Fever and won a WNBA Championship in 2012, was inducted into the Women's Basketball Hall of Fame and Naismith Memorial Basketball Hall of Fame Class in 2020, and she now serves as the Fevers' general manager. She was awarded the 2021 Freedom Award from the Indiana Civil Rights Commission in January for her work in the Indianapolis community — specifically, her Catch The Stars Foundation, which helps underprivileged youth pursue their dreams in a healthy learning environment.

So where do I fit in all of this? As a member of the Pacers Sports and Entertainment company, I act as the digital marketing coordinator for the Indiana Fever organization.

My job is to oversee the Fever's social media channels (Twitter, Instagram, Facebook, and YouTube). I am usually the one either pressing or scheduling our online posts.

With the rise of social media presence, I play a crucial role in getting our players' messages out to the masses across all social media platforms. It was a very rewarding summer for me in terms of personal growth. In my position, I got to amplify their voices. For example, we took advantage of media availabilities. These occur after games, practices, and community events. Players are required to answer questions from the local/national media, and during this past summer, our players would incorporate their thoughts on the racial inequality into their responses. If we had time after a media availability, Achonwa, for example, would come directly to me and tell me what she had on her mind, and we would get it posted immediately. We were not trying to hide anything. We wanted our players' voices to be out there as much as possible.

At the Black Lives Matter march in Indianapolis in June 2020, I took photos of the crowd and players marching and speaking. This was personally satisfying in terms of providing the platform for our players to share what they thought was important.

As a content creator, your goal is to disrupt somebody's feed and make them stop. People have a habit of just scrolling and scrolling, and you want them to stop on your posts.

In terms of the posts about "Black Lives Matter" and "Say Her Name," we wanted to disrupt someone and make them stop, but we also wanted be very educational and informative with our posts. For example, we posted graphics around voting season, encouraging our followers to vote. We provided a pull quote from Catchings on her mindset when it comes to voting and how important its relationship with our ongoing fight for equality really is. We aimed to touch them in an emotional way — either with a player's soundbite or best core graphics that make at least one person think, "Oh wow, I never thought about it that way."

Naturally, other users will disagree and speak out against your stance. When Colin Kaepernick took a knee during the national anthem, the Fever happened to kneel as well. At the time, there was plenty of poor reception from social media users and WNBA fans in general.

Since the summer and the 2020 WNBA season, I have seen firsthand the people's perspectives change. There has always been the loyal fan base that has stuck with the players since day one, but I have witnessed a significant change in terms of the casual fan: Somebody who did not know much about the WNBA but happened to love what they've been standing for and has jumped on board, becoming supporters.

To those who still remain defensive toward the topic of racial injustice, my one suggestion would be to simply listen and start conversations with those closest to you.

I started inner dialogue within my family and friends. My message to them was to actually hear people when they talk and share their experiences. Don't pretend and act like you actually hear what they're saying.

As an organization, the Fever are really hoping to educate the players on how to be advocates, where to focus their energy, and how to harness that energy and spark real change. It's great to speak on issues and be active on social media while the topic is popular, but now the fight must move to making real-life impact in the local communities and national media outlets.

For myself, my future will revolve around continuing the fight. I want to get more and more people to listen, and I think my profession gives me the perfect opportunity to do so. I want to continue to have conversations with my family, friends, and coworkers, so we can prepare ourselves to assist and support the individuals pressing the issue forward.

I know it's a pillar of belief in the Fever organization, the WNBA, and for myself, so it's not going away any time soon. The most important thing I've learned is being able to listen and recognize their perspectives. Once you do that, you can then relay those messages to your own life and serve as an ally in the ongoing fight.

CHAPTER 6: LET'S TALK ABOUT IT

JORDYN CARSWELL'S STORY AS TOLD TO ALEX SCHMITT

Key Words: Female, Collegiate-Women's Volleyball, Athlete, Race, Louisiana/Texas

The world is full of differences. There are those we perceive in ourselves, and those we perceive from others. Some are noticed early; some are noticed later in life. Others come after you are educated in how to see them. My life is defined by a lot of them, but I am the one who knows how to put it into words. And I am a perfectionist, so I like to know the best ways to do it to the best of my ability.

My name is Jordyn, and I'm a volleyball player for Louisiana Tech. I've been playing since I was young, and I traveled throughout the country playing. I also traveled throughout the country with my mom and my stepdad. We moved a lot for their work, so I was used to being mobile. But there were times I wished I was able to have a closer family. It may have helped me understand the world around me better.

I grew up a bit sheltered with a white mom and stepdad, but there was a difference between them and me. I am biracial, and so is my sister, Gabrielle. But even then, we're not the same color. She's a bit darker than I am. Those passing by us in the neighborhood would notice this difference too, highlighted every time someone asked our mother if we were adopted.

Our neighborhood had a pool, and it gets hot in Texas. So one day, when I was around 16, my friends and I wanted to go for a nice, cool dip in that pool. We walked to the gate, and I used my key to get in. But to make sure that no one was there who wasn't supposed to be there, a security guy was checking IDs.

He got to me, and he checked my ID but said that I was not allowed to go in.

"That's ridiculous! My mom is Tammy Stone! Just because she doesn't look like me or share the same name as me doesn't mean I'm not her daughter," is what I remember saying.

He didn't care, and he took my ID from me. Well, we eventually got in because my other friend lived down the street and that security guy let us through with them. I never saw him again after that, but neither did I see my ID.

Nor would this be the last time I would have a bad experience with someone.

When we got home after that incident, I didn't tell my mom what happened. I don't know whether I was embarrassed because it happened or if I was dreading the eventual hell my mom would have raised if she found out someone had mistreated her daughter. As I look back, I think it was a little combination of both.

Another time I had a brush with authority flexing their muscle was when my boyfriend and I were pulled over after going out for a night on the town.

We went to Minden, Louisiana, one evening, and we were enjoying our ride back at night. It was great to have some time together, and it felt good to take my mind off everything. The southern nights of Louisiana are rather nice. It's not too cool, and it's not too hot. It's a bit muggy at times, but the breeze from the window of the car was too good not to feel. But all the magic of the moment can be turned to dread whenever red-and-blue lights start flashing behind you.

It scared me — not just for my safety but for my boyfriend's. He's mixed just like me. When you're any shade of Black, driving a nice car, you're already viewed as a thousand stereotypes. None of which are helpful when you're being stopped by police.

So we pulled over, and the officer asked us to step out of the car. He and his partner separated us, and they asked us if there were any drugs or guns in the car. As I am being interrogated, two more cars pull up in full lights, and now it's four cars on the side of the road, lighting up the night like a rave.

Why were they pulling us over? Why were they asking about drugs and guns?

We're just two student-athletes enjoying a night out on the town. But now, it was just Suspect 1 and Suspect 2.

Ultimately, my boyfriend let them search the car, and, naturally, they found nothing because there was nothing. But since they didn't believe us, they figured they needed to make sure themselves. They let us go, but that doesn't take away the feeling of being perhaps one miscommunication away from watching my boyfriend become another statistic. It reminded me that there's two different realities we live in.

The difference is also present on the court.

When you step out on a volleyball court, you see the big difference in team diversity. There were a lot of white girls out there with a few Black teammates sprinkled here and there. My team was one of the few to have a very diverse supporting cast. But that diversity didn't stop the expectations that came with being mixed.

Because I'm part Black, I guess I am apparently supposed to jump higher, move faster, hit harder, and never run out of energy.

While all these traits did get me into a NCAA Division 1 school on an athletic scholarship, they weren't superpowers that I got just for being part Black. I worked hard to be the best. I busted my ass to go out and break my high school's record for most digs in a single game. I worked hard on hitting lines to get the highest hitting percentage on my team my sophomore, junior, and senior year. I was good because I put in the time. That's how I got to Louisiana Tech.

And that's where I met Coach McCray.

She came to coach us my sophomore year at Tech, and with that came a lot of teaching moments. She pulled the team aside and talked to us as a group, and she talked to us individually afterward. She teaches us a lot in how we can change the game on the court. The ones that really stuck with me were the ones she gave us off the hardwood.

Some of the things we talked about were small like how our hair is different. I always knew it was. I had to brush a lot and use different products and chemicals to keep it straight. I'd hardly dip into the pool just because I didn't want to have curls. I didn't see them as useful in my beauty standards. But after learning about where my beauty standards came from, I decided to go natural. No, I don't have a giant afro like you might see on old disco album covers. I let my hair come down in their natural curls. I only started letting it get curly in college. All the time before that, I was working hard to keep it straight and well-kept.

Another lesson was the ability to be accepted by both parts of who I am.

When you're biracial like me, you feel like you're in a sort of no-man's land. You have two people who love you but look different from you. Your parents and family look different than you, and they have different experiences than you. You feel like you have to pick a side — but that neither one really embraces you like you belong. The white girls weren't like me nor were the Black girls like me. I felt like I had something to say to the world around me, but no one would listen to me.

No one except Coach McCray.

After talking with her, I learned that I had a voice in all of this. I learned that I didn't have to watch from the sidelines while others played. I was able to let my voice ring out and have my stories told. I am able to better educate myself and others to the reality in which I live. It has helped me get through the talks with my mother about how I was brought up. It has helped me talk with my family about how I feel and live with the reality of the times.

The hardest thing to come of this is the difference my family has with the murder of George Floyd and its impact across the country.

My mom put up a video of my sister and me talking about how we felt about it, and a few family members shared what could be called at best "different views of reality." I felt like their views had come from a place of not knowing a lot about the subject but refusing to look further into the issue. That is one thing I hope to change in them as well as in others with my voice.

I feel like if I am able to start the conversation — whether it's with family or someone who wants to know a little more, I'll be able to help others see the world in which I live. I hope to change the hearts and minds of others, but I know that there will always be people you just can't change.

I just hope that through my education, I'm both able to better understand why people think the way they do but also how I can start the conversation with them. I believe that if people are able to talk, they are able to learn. And the only way you can teach them is if you can speak.

CHAPTER 7: COMMIT TO COASTAL

CJ ALLARD'S STORY AS TOLD TO
DR. ADAM J. KUBAN

Key Words: Male, Collegiate-Women's Volleyball, Assistant Coach, International-Student Rights, South Carolina/Massachusetts

The Netherlands.
Turkey.
Russia.
Argentina.
Denmark.
Hungary.
Croatia.
Israel.
Italy.
Serbia.
Greece.
Bulgaria.
Norway.
Brazil.
The Czech Republic.
And, of course, the USA.

I've coached collegiate volleyball players from across the globe, and I still find myself competing from time to time. Volleyball but also golf. I do love being on a golf course! Being an assistant coach for the indoor and beach volleyball teams at Coastal Carolina University just outside Myrtle Beach, South Carolina, I think I've found the sweet spot for these two sports.

Well, the geographic sweet spot — sure. But maybe not so much the climatic sweet spot on this particular mid-May day: It's 60 degrees outside, and that's just too cold! No way am I grabbing my clubs or hitting the beach when it's like this, so I think it's safe to say that, since I left the Midwest about six or seven years ago, I've become a true Southerner.

I love what I do and where I do it. Someday, I want to become a head coach. That's the goal, and I refuse to be out-worked by anybody. By other coaches. Even by my own players. I'll get out there with them during practice. Run some sprints. Hit a few balls. I'm only a couple years older than most of them, so why not? I hate losing more than I enjoy winning, and I think most of my players feel the same way, so, as part of my coaching philosophy, I'll tell them that our practices have to be harder, longer, tougher, more miserable ... We have to put in the time, effort, and energy now so that we peak when it matters the most.

And it works! We went 18-1 in Fall 2020, a unique season to say the least because of the COVID-19 global pandemic. I'm proud of my team. Everybody feels that intense, competitive pressure, but I've learned that for some, it's experienced differently than it is for others. Particularly for international student-athletes. Their path leading up to that opening-season match can be more difficult than for the American recruits.

For me, I sign annual contracts, and I make a livable wage each year with some fiscal incentives that can boost that income: athletes' GPAs, their academic progress rates, our overall team rank and its win-loss record. So there's that pressure on my side. I also get to travel, mainly across the Southeast USA, to recruit players and to promote our program and the University. It's my job to keep our program competitive.

Commit To Coastal.

That's my line — even tried to get the University to adopt it as its tagline.

But here's what I've noticed: Even if they're not from the Southeast, American athletes still feel at home here. The campus welcomes them with its red brick and white pillars, and there are palm trees everywhere. The people may be different, but the social expectations are similar. The accents might take some getting used to, but the language is the same. The food might be eclectic, but the shops and stores are familiar. The academic courses likely offer new ways of thinking, but you largely know what you're getting when you sign up for college.

This isn't the case for the international student-athletes.

For most, I'm the first American that they meet once they're off the plane and out of the airport. And by then, they've already faced challenges that my domestic athletes have not. For one, some of those countries don't want their best, brightest, most-athletic students leaving and coming to the USA to play. I mean, it kind of makes sense: The USA wouldn't want to lose its star athletes either. So some of those countries push back with some fear-mongering tactics to try to persuade their student-athletes to stay home. For example, maybe they won't guarantee them a spot on their national volleyball team after they've finished their studies in the USA and return home. Something like that — fear's a heck of a motivator.

Once I've convinced them to commit to Coastal, and once they've arrived, there's major culture shock. I can remember one athlete from Greece: I picked her up at the airport, and I still recall that wide-eyed look on her face. Kind of like a young child on Christmas morning, y'know, when you wake up and see the presents under the tree and stare in amazement because it did not look like that the night before.

So that same athlete: I remember taking her to WalMart and how she just gawked in the candy aisle. Among other things, I've learned from my international student-athletes that our array and abundance of candy is not replicated elsewhere in the world!

Once the culture shock subsides and it's time to look at academics, international student-athletes sometimes face inconsistent assessments from the NCAA, which has its own formula to translate academic rigor. Certain countries approach

31

early-childhood education and adolescent education differently than how we do it in the USA, so it's tough to determine just how prepared these athletes are for a college curriculum. Some get bored; the things they're learning in their college classes here in the States would've been covered at a much earlier age. Off the top of my head — foreign languages: Other countries have their students learning another language far earlier than we do in the States. On the other hand, English and US History, for example, can be very challenging subjects for first-semester international student-athletes for reasons I'm sure you can imagine.

So I push them to work with their respective academic advisors to take, at least early on, courses in math, science, and physical ed. Scientific concepts and mathematical equations are consistent from one country to the next, and as athletes, they're usually comfortable academically in a class devoted to exercise and fitness.

College-curriculum vocabulary can also be a challenge to decipher. In my experience, I've found international student-athletes struggle to navigate certain idiosyncrasies and jargon: What is a credit hour? Why do some courses have prerequisites? How is a BA different than a BS?

In general, I've noticed that, similar to American recruits, my international players have the same "butterflies" or concerns when they start college: How will I handle being on my own for the first time? Are my classes going to be manageable? How many new people will I meet? Will I be able to prove myself to my new volleyball teammates? But those international student-athletes have additional thoughts and anxieties that I don't think people realize: I'm in a new country ... this is the first time that I haven't been around anybody who speaks my native language ... the food is really different here ... the people here are nicer, more outgoing, but also louder ... when will I be able to see my family again?

And then compound these concerns and anxieties with your academic classes, weight-room sessions, athletic-training sessions, plus professors and administrators who expect you to pull it all together and keep it all together for four seasons.

I certainly didn't get into coaching to become an advocate for international student-athletes. Instead, I accepted the job at Coastal Carolina because it was an opportunity to advance my career. I knew the head coach was Hungarian, and I knew there were international players on the roster, but I couldn't have foreseen the impact that these women would have on me personally and professionally. I've gotten many thank-you notes and letters from past players, telling me how helpful I've been and what that meant to them. That, in turn, means a lot to me.

Moving forward, regardless of where my career path takes me, I'll keep open the international recruiting lines in order to try and help future international volleyball prospects live their dream. Through these recruitments, I'll help ensure that their path to an American college degree is set up for success, and I hope that other coaches adopt a similar desire to help our sport's international players. Often, it seems that people just put students into categories based on checked boxes such as their major, their GPA, their demographic identities, and so forth. Honestly, I think the best change that could happen for these athletes is for those who work at universities to become more informed about what it's like to be an international student-athlete. A small, up-front investment into making an international student-athlete's journey more accessible can have such a positive impact on that young person and create ripple effects for their success long into the future.

CHAPTER 8: FROM MY SEWING TO OUR SEWING

MARUTI CHAURAN'S STORY AS TOLD TO ZEKE HANSEN (WITH TRANSLATION ASSISTANCE PROVIDED BY PRIYANKA KALE)

Key Words: Male, Youth-Soccer, Coach, Gender Equality/Poverty,
(International) India/England

Hamari Silai is a term in Hindi that means "Our Sewing." My friend, Mohan Rathod, and I started our organization Hamari Silai to empower women from a low-income background by providing them with job opportunities. We encourage women to become self-reliant by providing stitching and tailoring skills. Hamari Silai offers activities where women learn to manufacture and design sport jerseys, polo shirts, custom uniforms, eco-friendly sanitary napkins, and other traditional dresses.

There are many organizations in our slum community of Ambedkar Nagar, Colaba (in Mumbai, India) that focus on other people and topics, but there are not many that focus on women only. Many women here work hard in places like the fish markets, where they spend long hours on their knees cleaning fish and risking their health by working without gloves. In addition to the hazards, the fish market does not provide good pay.

Since women here do not receive the same basic education and they are not taught the same skills as men, they do not have a real opportunity at working in a full-time job that will pay them well. When women attend the workshops at Hamari Silai, it is not guaranteed that they will leave with that type of a job, but what they will leave with is confidence and empowerment, and that is our central goal with Hamari Silai.

Often, they do leave with more than just confidence, however. They leave with possibilities and capabilities they did not previously have. Many women have been able to make money off of the tailoring skills we have taught them by selling the cotton bags and masks they make. That alone makes good money compared to the fish market. Some women have come back to work full-time with Hamari Silai or other organizations that work in partnership with us. Some women do get jobs that are typically only held by men.

We hope that the women who come in here are able to teach what they learned in our centers to their daughters, so that those girls can go out and obtain the jobs they wouldn't have been able to otherwise had their mother not received the education they got from Hamari Silai.

This education is simple, but it's important.

It includes basic literacy, where they learn to write their name and read. It also includes banking transactions. Since young girls are forced into child marriage and often end up in child labor, they are stripped of the opportunity to learn those life skills. We think that by providing the 150 women we have now with these skills, it will end up being many more women who benefit from our work. There is a cycle that we want to continue with this organization.

It is a cycle that Mohan and I have been a part of.

We benefited from being a part of this as children in the OSCAR Foundation, which operates in the same area of Mumbai as we do. What the OSCAR Foundation does is they provide football (soccer) and basic education — things like literacy and basic math skills —

to children in the slums. Mohan and I went through that program as children and eventually got the opportunity to receive youth training so that we could become part of the OSCAR Foundation as coaches.

I remember it was quite funny going from being a player to being a coach. As a player, you are working with other boys your age and you have adult coaches, but when you become a young coach, you are coaching many young children at once. It is quite the difference! From these experiences in both playing and coaching football (soccer), Mohan and I have learned about the value of hard work, dedication, and fair competition. It is those qualities that we hope to pass on to these women, so they can pass on to other women and multiply the impact.

Being a coach for the OSCAR Foundation, I had the opportunity to go to the United Kingdom. It was through visiting other countries that I began to fully see how women in India were mistreated. You begin to think of the women in your life: your mother, your sisters, other friends, and other relatives. You see how they were impacted by this. Not only did I want to do this for the women but also for myself. I want to make an impact of my own, outside of the OSCAR Foundation, and because of my previous social work as a football (soccer) coach, I have the skills and training I need to continue Hamari Silai.

Part of extending the impact of this project is not only educating the women but also educating the men.

The women can feel empowerment, but for them to reap the benefits, the men have to respect that empowerment. It's because of this that Hamari Silai also has workshops for men, particularly the husbands of the women we have here. At these workshops, we teach them how to treat children and how to handle money. We also tell them that it is OK for the women to make decisions. Due to the patriarchal system in India, it is custom for the man to make the decisions for the family no matter how small the decision may seem. It has been one of our goals to change this.

For example, there was a husband of one of the women who didn't want his wife leaving the house to go and learn, especially if it was a long distance away. It was through our workshops that he was taught the importance of his wife being able to be self-reliant and confident by seeing how this equality has benefited others. He eventually became comfortable with letting her leave the house to pursue equal opportunity through Hamari Silai.

Situations like that is more of the typical change we see. It is not a big impact, at least not yet, but we are slowly breaking the gender stereotypes.

Once you start breaking down the stereotypes, it becomes easier to keep going. It is all a part of the cycle. Inequality will continue without these women and men who enter Hamari Silai sharing the knowledge that they receive. Change requires the women taking what they have learned from Hamari Silai to their daughters. Change requires the men to see a different perspective and to share that with their sons and their friends.

It requires "mere silai," or my sewing, to become "hamari silai."

CHAPTER 9: MAKING THE WORLD 1% SAFER

SCOTTY LEE'S STORY AS TOLD TO JOHN LYNCH

Key Words: Male, Youth-Soccer, Coach, Disability/Poverty/War, (International) Bosnia/Cambodia/Iraq/Colombia

Are you 1% better than you were yesterday?

It's a question I ask of both myself and the people I coach. Can you be 1% better than you were yesterday? If you can, then you'll be just fine.

That's my approach: as a coach, as a person, as a philanthropist. What you've done and what you are doing now aren't relevant to my mission as a trainer: It's what you dedicate yourself to doing tomorrow.

That philosophy serves me well in my work. The world, quite frankly, is pretty much shit. The fact is, my generation, the Gen Xers and Baby Boomers of the world, have fucked up the world for the people coming after us. Climate change, polarized politics, all of that? Us. Those poor bastards following us are going to have to experience the end result of all of our mistakes.

My organization, Spirit of Soccer, tries to make the world that 1% better every day. There are a lot of problems the organization has solved since we started in 1996, but the biggest one is landmine awareness. See, when our militaries go into foreign countries, we have a nasty habit of leaving behind some pretty bad consequences — landmines being one of the worst of them.

It's a problem that children in particular in these countries — including Iraq, Bosnia, Sri Lanka, and half a dozen more — face more than anyone else. Kids are losing their lives and bodies to landmine-related incidents every day, and it's largely because they don't know any better.

That's where I come in.

Soccer's pretty accessible as far as sports go: All you need is a ball, a couple goals, and enough people and space to play it. It's also popular across the whole world, so getting communities on board with our education program for landmine avoidance is usually pretty easy.

My first experience with the chaos that war can bring was in Bosnia. I had spent plenty of time in the country during the height of its civil war in 1993 delivering food convoys as part of Arsenal F.C.'s humanitarian efforts in the area, but my first experience with landmine removal wouldn't come for a couple more years. There was nothing left in Bosnia after the war, so while I was still coaching for Arsenal F.C. in 1996, the Club sent me down to Sarajevo to do some coaching in the area to reintroduce the soccer programs the region had lost to the war. Turns out, the two main stadiums in the city were heavily mined. Thankfully, I had some pretty damn good connections at the United Nations as a result of Arsenal's humanitarian partnership, which got the fields de-mined relatively quickly.

That wasn't the end of that exposure to the threat of landmines. While I was there, some kids were playing a game of soccer, and a ball went out of bounds into some tall grass. They tripped a fragmentation mine, which is used for anti-personnel purposes in war zones, killing them.

They never had a chance — the blast just tore them apart. That '96 trip to Bosnia lasted two months. What I saw changed my life.

39

See, as a coach, I know the importance of training. In sports, training is necessary at every level of development. You don't grow or progress without training, and that's exactly what we do for kids who might be the victim of landmines one day. We pair the messaging the kids need to hear with a universal messenger: the game of soccer.

That year, I founded Spirit of Soccer to make sure what I saw wouldn't happen again. I developed a Mine Risk Education program that could be applied through the training and coaching techniques of soccer, secured some funding from the U.S. State Department's Office for Weapons Removal and Abatement, and got to work building the organization. Twenty-five years later, it's still going strong, operating on four continents — Asia, Africa, South America, and Europe.

The way we get messaging to stick is pretty simple really: We play a game, and then we teach them a lesson. We'll alternate drills, lessons on the game, and full games with lessons on how to identify and avoid landmines. There are four pillars to our education program: "Keep Away. Don't Touch. Report. Communicate." It's simple for a reason; not only does it have to be easy to understand for children, but we encourage local coaches to pick up the program and keep teaching it.

The great thing about working within the coaching framework is that it allows us to keep our team small and efficient while still reaching plenty of people. One or two coaches can teach about 100 kids in a two-hour session, and the results speak for themselves. We've reached an estimated 60,000 children through our operations in Iraq alone, and we reach approximately 100,000 kids each year through not only the training programs but the tournaments and games that we set up in the area.

That's not just coach-speak either. My training methods have worked all over the world; Spirit of Soccer has done some amazing work in Cambodia, Iraq, and Colombia in 2005, 2007, and 2015, respectively. When I started Spirit of Soccer, international landmine deaths were over a thousand annually, and around 40% of those deaths were among children. Last year, the number of deaths was four, and the rate of landmine incidents in places we have visited is down 50%. It's not all because of us — landmine removal and decreased use of mines play a big part — but we're extremely proud of our results.

But it's a classic coaching technique: I come along; I engage you with something you love, and I educate you and then you leave and make better decisions.

Now, our mission is bigger than just landmine-awareness education. We've realized our platform is big enough and successful enough that we can start rolling other programs into our training. For example, advancing women's rights, spreading knowledge about climate change, and educating less fortunate areas about COVID-19 prevention have become big components of our latest curriculum.

We've been able to achieve a near-50-50 split between male and female coaches within our program, and, unsurprisingly, even in areas where women's rights are far behind the rest of the world, placing women in places of influence helps change perceptions of how women can function and be treated in their communities. Even in deeply fundamentalist Islamic communities, particularly where the Taliban are our main points of contact in terms of government, putting women in leadership positions has opened eyes to what women can do. It's all about the game where performance on the field is all that matters. We hope to get that 50-50 balance to reflect itself in the kids we coach in the coming years too.

So back to the original question. Are you 1% better than you were yesterday? I certainly hope I am. The whole point of Spirit of Soccer is to make the world a better, safer place. I hope that counts for more than 1%.

CHAPTER 10: MORE THAN A GAME

DAN LEVENTHAL'S STORY AS TOLD TO BAYLEN HITE

Key Words: Male, Youth-Lacrosse, Coach, Poverty/Race, New York

Where we come from, only 14% of the adults in Highbridge, a neighborhood located in the heart of the Bronx (New York), have graduated with a college degree. The average per capita income is just over $17,000 per year. Our kids have a very tough upbringing, and that is an understatement. They have seen more and been through more than I ever have, and while I know and they know that I can't replicate that, I think trust is the biggest thing that I can bring.

My earliest lacrosse memory is 3rd grade, just juggling the ball with a stick that was way too big for me. My dad played a little bit in high school, and while I played other sports in high school, lacrosse just seemed to be the one where I fell in love. It gave me everything; it gave me my drive, and it gave me goals to reach. Lacrosse allowed me to get an education that I would have never gotten or even been in consideration for. That's what I want to do for our kids, and I want to help create that with Bronx Lacrosse.

While Bronx Lacrosse is obviously about the sport, its main focus is education. Our athletes are truly students to the closest degree. We have enhanced classes, extra study time, and tutors who help mentor our kids. Then we use the sport as a vessel and try to bring in more kids who want to play the sport.

When the kids are hooked on the sport, that's when we introduce them to the meaning of the program and the educational value that it truly is.

Our students are allowed to play based on their academic performance. We have weekly check-ins with the kids, making sure they have been attending all their classes and keeping up with their homework. If one of these categories starts to slip, then we work with the them — but we may take away lacrosse if the situation doesn't improve. We want education to be at the forefront because we know that while your time in athletics can run out, education is what will carry you. That is our focus as educators and as leaders for our students.

No program is without challenges, and when you lead a program — especially a lacrosse program with kids from the Bronx — many of whom are African Americans or children of color, these challenges hit you right in the face when you go to a game. The "looks" start right when we bring our teams to tournaments and matches.

Most of the sport is exclusively white kids. In fact, only 18% of collegiate athletes in men's lacrosse are African American or people of color. This is a stigma that we are trying to break across the sport.

While it's not easy to come in and make these changes, we feel with the reach of Bronx Lacrosse, we are starting to turn the corner with diversity in the sport.

We start to think about the sport of lacrosse and then mix that with the emotions our country faced this past summer in 2020. It becomes very easy to see why this is so important, and this means so much more than just the game. Being a white man in a leadership position of so many students and athletes of color, I feel like the best thing I can do is listen. Just stop and listen...

Listening is so hard for some people, yet we learn the most when we just stop and listen.

I hear the stories from my students whether that's adversity, racism, or issues because of their background. You really start to see the bigger picture. It's not just in lacrosse but in sports as a whole, and you start to understand why these games mean so much more.

Just like I was saying with education, sports can be a vessel for so much more change, equality, and education. It's so much more than just a game.

That's where I want to see Bronx Lacrosse go and where I think it can go. Together, we can make a difference in these children's lives and not just in the present but in the future as well.

Now for the age-old question: Where exactly do we take that? Where do we go with this program to help continue to impact and change kids' lives? Well, it starts with fundraising. We need to be able to get this equipment in the hands of our kids at no cost. This will help us build on our mission of empowering kids beyond the game of lacrosse. And so far, we have run fundraising efforts in our community with great success. Even in spite of the recent pandemic, we had a community food drive this past winter. This was to ensure our community — where we take so much pride — could get the food they needed for the holidays.

Along with continued fundraising efforts, we need to continue to develop as educators and continue to grow as leaders to help our kids reach their goals. I also think we need to listen more. Just like I said earlier, I and others like me haven't faced the same challenges that many of our kids have gone through. The only way to give them our all is to listen and learn from them in order to craft a better way of teaching in our program.

All in all, the progress in sports is working; the process is working, and these are all things that I feel Bronx Lacrosse has built on. We want to be able to help our athletes sustain themselves past the game of lacrosse and well into their futures. But we have to do more than just what the game requires to do that. Through Bronx Lacrosse, I feel as though we have created a pretty good start to that process.

CHAPTER 11: SPEAKING FROM THE HEART

RYAN "ROCK" PERROTTE'S STORY AS TOLD TO RYAN KLIMCAK

Key Words: Male, Collegiate-Men's Volleyball, Coach, Race, Indiana/ (International) Canada

"You are in a position of influence, and you should do it," my mother said.

I had done hours of research. I was anxious, and I was neurotic.

Following the death of George Floyd, the AVCA (American Volleyball Coaches Association) asked me to give a presentation to other volleyball coaches about how to talk about race among their teams and players.

A fellow coach contacted me (who's a good friend of mine) to inquire what I was planning to discuss. After informing him what I was planning to present based on my historical research, he told me that coaches really wanted to know how to talk to players about race because a lot of collegiate men's volleyball teams are not racially diverse in the United States.

I took all my notes and chucked them out and ended up using just my historical recollection and speaking from the heart. With the presentation through Zoom due to the COVID-19 pandemic, I wanted to make sure others were comfortable talking about a highly sensitive issue.

Growing up in Canada, it was a culture shock moving to the United States to attend college to play volleyball. As someone who grew up surrounded by a lot of different cultures, coming to America was like entering a warped time zone. There was so much variety in my life — from different nationalities, different religions, and different viewpoints. My mother, who recently passed away, would say, "Listen, you are a young Black male growing up in the west side of Windsor, Ontario, Canada. These are some things that you need to do to ensure that you have an opportunity to make a better life for yourself."

Education was at the forefront.

During my first year of college, I worked at a factory supply plant back home in the summer. This wonderful Polish woman I had worked with, who came to Canada from the old Eastern Bloc (former Eastern European communist countries) with her family to flee communism, once remarked when I told her that I was Roman Catholic:

"I did not know there were Black Catholics."

This comment was really interesting to me, but I did not take any offense to it whatsoever. She had never experienced or interacted with a Black Catholic before. I remember telling my grandmother later that winter when I saw her, and she laughed. My grandmother used to ask me all the time if I would marry a white person or a Black person. I quipped jokingly, "A white Protestant," and she would laugh and ask why. I said because if you could get a white Protestant and Black Catholic to unionize, then there would finally be peace in the world!

My mother was born on a small Caribbean island, Grenada, and when she wanted to study nursing, she moved to London, England. They were going through their social revolution in the 1950s and 1960s. She mentioned to me on a few occasions, in terms of education or schooling, the opportunities she was afforded or not afforded because of the color of her skin. After completing her studies in London, she moved to Brooklyn, New York. When she made the decision to move to Canada, she became the first Black registered nurse at Brantford General Hospital. She then moved to Windsor, Ontario, and became the first Black registered nurse in 1967 at Hotel-Dieu of St. Joseph Hospital, where she would work for three decades.

It was not easy for her at times dealing with some of the administration or even behaviors of patients as a Black woman trying to heal, comfort, and do God's work.

My mother told me, "You have to be very careful because not everybody is accepting." My mother taught me how to overcome adversity throughout her entire life.

Learning these experiences growing up, I understood our original sin in Canada was, in some ways, different from that of the United States. The original sin of Canada was the taking of land from the natives, then creating residential schools that took children away from the natives or Aboriginal families in the 19th century, and then trying to assimilate them into "Canadian" culture.

The biggest difference, in my opinion, between the USA and Canada is that we had the opportunity to learn and talk about the history of our country's inception in detail, whereas in the United States, that isn't always the case. I was taught about history at both my primary and secondary schools.

As a coach, I want my players to be global citizens after graduation, so I believe it is important to talk to them about world affairs pertaining to cultures.

I don't think I, nor my predecessor, started out deliberately recruiting kids from all over, but our roster is full of kids from all over the world. They come from Puerto Rico, South America, Europe, and even Canada. Diversity makes us better humans, and even though my players are young kids maturing into adults, they're curious about the world they find themselves in. We do have conversations often as a team about diversity and cultures.

In the aftermath of the death of George Floyd, I knew what was going on in America: a racial reckoning for justice and life. As a coach, it was important for me to allow an open forum to discuss difficult topics with my team so they could freely express their thoughts and feelings.

I cannot say whether or not the team got closer together — only they can, but I sure hope that was the case. It brought understanding to a very serious subject matter, which had been put on hold for so long.

We need to learn to accept and learn from other people — to accept them for who they are!

In addition to having open discussions with my team, I was contacted by another coach to give a presentation on race in front of fellow volleyball coaches the American Volleyball Coaches Association.

This was the presentation I gave:

I discussed the history of this country when it comes to race but also how I have never had a racial incident during my 44 years involved in volleyball. This is an inclusive game, and I wanted to stress the point that even though a lot of teams may not have a lot of diversity, it does not make you a racist just because you have never interacted with somebody of a different culture or a different race. We are all capable of learning about each other as long as we are willing to listen and there is a dialogue. My final point was just that: Simply communicating with players honestly on your team helps bridge the understanding.

"What are your experiences dealing with race?"

"What was your upbringing like when it comes to race?"

"Did you have a multi-racial school?"

"Were other races on your teams growing up, and what was that interaction like with people who are not the same as you?"

All of which were questions I wanted to illustrate in how to communicate to their teams. All to encapsulate getting to know their players and their cultures.

I received some texts and phone calls from coaches immediately following the presentation. Many were very thankful; others were relieved knowing how to finally approach the subject. What presumably started as a tense (perhaps even uncomfortable) feeling among those listening to the presentation hopefully changed.

It doesn't matter if you are white or Black or any other shade in between. You have to be proud of who you are and what you represent. We should not have guilt for who we become and who we are.

I have a particularly vivid memory where a Black custodial worker approached me after a match in Irvine, California. He came up to me and started talking.

"I just wanted to shake your hand," he said.

I shook his hand, and it was almost like he was in tears.

"I didn't know there were Black coaches in volleyball," the man stated.

This interaction was really profound. I was really proud of this moment, and moments like this carry a lot of weight.

CHAPTER 12: GIVING LIFE LESSONS

MATT CRENSHAW'S STORY AS TOLD TO ZACH GUNN

Key Words: Male, Collegiate-Men's Basketball, Coach, Race, Virginia/Texas/Maryland/Indiana/ (International) Germany

From the time I was a young kid, I was always on the move from city to city and, in some cases, moving to separate countries. Originally from Virginia, but I've had stops in Texas, Maryland, and even Germany. I came from a military family since my mom and grandma, who were both very monumental in my life, each served some time in the military. Moving from these cities and countries at such a young age helped shaped me and helped me be able to connect with a variety of different people who came from unique backgrounds.

Growing up in Germany was an exceptional experience. As you can imagine, I was one of the few African American kids in the area, and one thing I picked up at an early age is racism is a taught action. It helped shape me and connect me with several people as well as be comfortable in different situations no matter the circumstance. A lot of life lessons and experiences were gained throughout my time being in these different areas.

Coming from a military background, I felt the need to carry the torch, so out of college, I decided to join the Navy too. The experiences I had in the Navy are memories that I will carry with me for a lifetime. I was able to establish relationships with all races and ethnicities of people, and I take pride in that. A majority of these experiences were positive, but with that being said, there were some negatives too. I was able to turn those negatives into life lessons and make the most out of the situation.

As an African American man who grew up around other races, ethnicities, and backgrounds, I feel I have a unique skill to connect with people and be a leader in society. I will always try to bring individuals together and unite them.

One person who had an everlasting impact on my life and one of the reasons I am so passionate for racial injustice is my grandmother. She's a very special person to me and is somebody whom I look up to dearly. She has done so much for our family, and I can only aspire to be like her. She endured so much in her life, and a lot of that included overcoming discrimination and racial inequality. In her time, she was able to provide for a family of five children, which would have been crazy to imagine in the era she was doing it and her circumstances. She was an extremely hard worker, and seeing this at a young age always left a perpetual effect on me and was very inspirational. The way she was eager to always put others first and her passion to give back is something that I try to do myself.

Along with my grandmother, my mom was a massive role model to me. My father passed away when I was 3 years old, so everything was on my mom's plate from there with the help from my grandma too at times. Seeing everything she had to endure caused me to grow up and mature younger than most kids are used to at such an early stage. For my brother and me, while growing up, we saw how hard both my grandma and mom worked. My grandma was always putting other people's needs first. For instance, during the week, she was always caring for others as she worked at an Emergency Center in Virginia. During weekends, she spent her time in the community and always tried to give back in some sort of fashion, and to see that at an early age is something I have absolutely tried to replicate as I have gotten older and been around the young men whom I coach.

Not only did I have my mother and grandma to lean on, but I had other mentors, including Coach Billie Gillespie and my military Coach

Al Young. These two showed me what mentorship and coaching is about, and I try to model what they did for me as young man growing up to the current young men I am around. These are two people whom I feel like I could go to whenever I needed somebody to talk to or just needed some good advice. Coach Young specifically was always willing to push my limits and try to get the best out of me as an athlete and person. The relationships we built are something I pride myself in, and they — without question — showed me what being a good mentor is about and how to have strong relationships.

When I first started coaching, I felt more like a brother to the players I had, but now, I am feeling more like an uncle and father figure for my players. The relationship aspect is something I take very seriously, and I want my guys to know that's always bigger than basketball.

At the end of the day and in any way that I can, I want to educate them in life. I want them to know that I will always be someone who can be counted on. For my players, I want them to see the positive impact I try to have on others, and I want them to carry out those same actions in their respective communities.

One reason that makes me so passionate about racial injustice is due to the fact that I am an African American man and have experienced racism firsthand in many situations throughout my life. Along with that, I am just naturally passionate about the subject as it hits close to home for me.

I have been the recipient of unfair behavior, so it is personal in many instances.

Not only that, but I have two Black sons who are starting their life as independent adults, so I want them to be aware of what society may be like for them as they get older. Aside from everything I have experienced personally, I am still at times angry that I have to worry about injustices happening to my sons or just to anybody in general. It is very frustrating because I was born in a different era, and yet we seem to still be dealing with the same problems. People will say it has gotten better when, in reality, it does not seem like there has been true change.

It can become tiring at times to ask yourself where the progress is. It is something that is in my everyday life that I have to deal with, and so because of that, it becomes a passion.

One way to go about this desired change and to see actual action is how you carry yourself.

To start off, you have to be a person of action. You cannot say one thing and then believe in another. Along with that, try to give back to communities of color. As an African American man, I know it is important that I go back to some of these communities and try to be a positive influence. Knowing I am constantly around young men, primarily African American men, it is vital that I am a good role model and educate them on a lot of these social-injustice issues that are currently going on in our society. It is crucial that I share what I know and do anything I can that can help regarding the topic of racial equality.

When these incidents over the summer involved with George Floyd occurred, it was something that hit home and was close to me. I have been in that position before as an African American man who has been stopped by the police and put into handcuffs and sat on the curb.

That is one of the most embarrassing feelings you can experience as a human being, sitting there as people are just looking at you in disgust.

And that is just one incident where I have experienced racial discrimination from the police. There have been a couple occasions where I have run into the police, and unfortunately, I have had to fear about what might take place in that situation. Never should anybody — regardless of race — have to worry about whether or not they will make it home in that instance.

It could have been me who became a statistic if something had gone wrong.

Not only has it been encounters with the police where I have experienced racism or unfair treatment but also my days in the Navy and just everyday life as an African American man too. Being an African American man in today's generation does not come easy as there are many obstacles that can be challenging.

You have to have uncomfortable conversations in order to get past these differences, and this is something I undoubtedly try to instill in my guys whom I coach. Like my former coaches, I have always had an open-door policy when it comes to things that are in relation to racial injustice. Being around the younger generation, I believe it is important that I can be a constant, positive influence, and that I guide them, instilling within them a positive outlook.

CHAPTER 13: ACCEPTING YOUR MENTAL HEALTH

TREY MOSES' STORY AS TOLD TO THOMAS "TC" DECKARD

Key Words: Male, Collegiate-Men's Basketball, Athlete, Mental Health, Indiana

I remember just looking over at Zach, smiling and laughing. I thought, "Wow, this is the happiest I had ever seen him."

It was my 20th birthday party, and I was thinking things were starting to change, and he was starting to take that next step. Honestly, that's what made my entire birthday: seeing his happiness. I can clearly remember it now. To see all my close friends there and to see him smiling — one of those smiles that lights up a room. It was just amazing to see. That night made having what happened so quickly after so much more difficult.

The next day, I woke up to four missed calls and two voicemails from Zach. In a rush to get to my morning classes, I decided to hold off on listening to them and stop by Zach's after class. When I got to his place, it was there I had discovered he had taken his life.

It was jarring how my life changed in under 24 hours.

The night before, he had seemed so happy. He'd had a rough time in the past, and it had taken a toll on his mental health, which is why his happiness the night prior had made my entire evening. Mental-health struggles were something he and I shared, especially after my clinical diagnosis my freshman year at Ball State. I had known he struggled himself, and my openness with my own struggles allowed him to have someone to talk to, and we were able to form a bond tighter than the one we had on the basketball court. It wasn't until the last six to eight months of his life that I noticed he was struggling a little more than he'd originally let on.

Personally, I think depression and anxiety — they're the type of things that can vary in terms of context. Is it, "Am I just sad? Am I just waking up sad *today?*" "Am I just nervous about this or that?" I feel that he may have just not truly known what was going on and having some personal issues of his own only added into that struggle.

Our dialogue about mental health only grew in May of my sophomore year when I had tried to take my own life. A few days after, he asked me why I hadn't told him how I was feeling. I told him I should've talked to him, and it honestly made me feel bad that I hadn't shared how I'd been feeling. Sharing all these personal issues, our friendship only grew. Then on the night he took his life, I'd received those missed calls and voicemails, and it left me with a sense of regret. I recalled when I had tried to take my own life, and he'd asked why I hadn't reached out, and then in his time of need, he'd reached out, but I just wasn't there.

It was hard for me to deal with that weight then, and sometimes I still deal with it now. It's just I need to understand that I shouldn't beat myself up over it.

We had a coach who would say, "We'd walk barefoot to Alaska and back to have Zach back." That applies to me personally because I would do whatever to be able to go back and answer one of those calls.

I made it my mission after he took his life to dedicate everything I did in his honor. I felt it was my responsibility to dedicate everything I did to Zach. Especially after what he said in those voicemails. When I listened to them after that tragic night, I heard a constant message of what he wanted me to be. He wanted me to be successful in basketball;

he wanted me to be successful in life. I think the biggest thing I took away is I could relate to the pain he was feeling. I could hear it.

Through those voicemails, I could feel what he was going through. And it was tough to hear. If I had answered the phone, I wonder if he'd still be here today. I've kind of gotten over that stage, but it's still hard: hearing how much he loved me, how much he cared about me, how much he wanted me to be successful in life and on the court, and how much he wanted me to keep going no matter what. It was also understanding that life isn't easy, but it's so much better with people who truly love and care about you. I know he's one person who genuinely loved and cared about me no matter what I did for him.

I changed my basketball number from 41 to his 24, and I've got a tattoo on my finger of '241', which is a combination of both our numbers, to honor him.

I enjoyed our memories on the court as well. Zach never really had an opportunity to show his intensity, but there was one time in practice where he revealed his ferocity. We were doing this one-on-one drill, and he and I were on different baskets. For some reason, I looked over at his basket, and he's hardcore dunking on someone. That was an awesome moment that still lingers in my memory.

To honor him further, I started a foundation, 24 Reasons, which is dedicated to mental-health awareness and accepting your issues and learning to live with them. One of my favorite things about my foundation is how much I've been able to help others. I love it when someone reaches out to me and says they've been struggling recently, but then they see their 24 Reasons shirt or bracelet, and they'll be reminded to keep going and that it's okay to not be okay. Through my foundation, I hope to inspire people to find their own reasons, and if they can't, they can always reach out to me — reach out to anyone — for help. The biggest thing I always say is, "It's okay not to be okay" because that's better than not being here.

I feel over time that mental health has been an issue many men have been taught not to speak about and to keep quiet. It comes from a mindset of previous generations to just "shrug it off." There was the attitude that men aren't allowed to cry that has created a stigma around this topic. A lot of these perceptions have been taught to both men and women in sports through mindsets and behaviors of their coaches. The influence they hold sort of implies to the young athletes — and to people in general — to not show weakness or vulnerability and to just power through it all. Fortunately, though, you now have men and women both speaking out on these topics and vocalizing that it is okay to talk about these types of issues. Talking about it and allowing the younger generations to see that it is okay to feel a certain way allows the deconstruction of the stigma around mental health.

I passionately feel that accepting your own issues is the first threshold to cross in learning to live with them. I feel that so many people are in denial, and acceptance is crucial to dealing with mental-health challenges. I remember through high school I hadn't heard about anyone taking their own life or being depressed, but as I got older, that changed.

My freshman year, I saw stuff on Twitter about depression, and I thought to myself, "There's no way. That's not what I'm going through. Not me. Sure, I've been sad. I've cried. But that's not me; I don't have these issues." Then I get diagnosed with depression, and it changed to, "Maybe this *is* me. Maybe this is what I'm going through."

I feel that the hardest yet most important part is admitting and accepting your own issues. Then I feel the next step is sharing your issues with those closest to you. I have my own way of sharing my issues, and your way may be different, but it is still important to share with those important to you. We all need people. We are all put here to love and care for others, so I feel, after personal acceptance, that sharing with those around you about your issues is incredibly important. Once you're able to accept and share your issues, you're going to find it much easier to find your reasons to keep going.

Chapter 14: Finding the Light

Jugman Dhami's Story as Told to Cooper Griffin

Key Words: Male, Collegiate-Boxing/Soccer, Athlete, Mental Health, Indiana/Illinois

Twelve rounds. Three minutes a piece. More goes into these three minutes than you think. Anger, rage, sadness. Without the ring, I hold all of these things inside. But in the ring, those three things are channeled into my fists. These things motivate me to do what I do. When I put those things into my fists and force them out, they don't captivate my head. Boxing gives me relief nothing else can.

Boxing is something for me that solves a lot of my problems in a healthy way.

There is something about winning in boxing that makes it different than anything I have ever experienced. Even in soccer, I never got the same gratification that I do winning in the ring. When I'm in the ring, it's all me. It's me against the guy in front of me. I get to see how all of my work pays off. When I'm boxing, I take all of the training, knowledge, and experience, and I put it into one performance. I manifest all of the success.

I won my first fight ever. I got a big head after that. "Well, this shit's easy!"

I came back, and my coach said he had another fight for me. I got there, and it was a skinny white dude who I thought I could destroy. Little did I know he had been fighting for 10 years. I went at him for three rounds. Relentlessly. All of a sudden, I got tired and he knew that. He whooped my ass after that. It was non-stop. He hit me everywhere, and I couldn't do anything about it.

I didn't want to box for a month.

When you get hit hard, that shows a lot about your character. The question is: Can you take that pain and use it and get the job done? Mentally, I have taken a lot of pain. With boxing, I know nobody can beat me in my head. I've used the pain to callous my mind to be tougher. But physically, I've learned a lot from getting my ass beat. There is something about getting hit that teaches your body. If I get hit in the ribs 500 times, the next time somebody tries it, I am definitely going to know I need to block it. You can't callous your ribs, so I've used the pain to learn how to react. I've learned to use that method in all aspects of my life.

Life can take more than it gives.

The night is only 12 hours, and after that 12 hours, life is full of sunlight. But those 12 hours of darkness can be intimidating.

Sometimes those 12 hours can feel like an eternity. That's when depression starts to be an issue. Depression is a hole you just can't get out of. Or at least it's very hard. It's a feeling that no matter what you do, you can't claw your way out. You can't sleep. You can't eat. You can't do anything.

A lot of times, people put themselves in situations that stress them out and call it depressed. Laziness and irritation are not always equivalent to depression. They can contribute to it, but some people project it. People do it so much that it feels like it's a trend.

They hear these sad artists put out thoughtful music and think that is the cool thing to identify with. They choose to manifest something that hurts. But for people who really struggle, it's a lot deeper than that.

For people who really struggle with depression... they need a big change. That change might be from the outside, but a lot of times, it has to come from within.

I grew up in Chicago and moved to a small town called Connersville in Indiana. Back in those times, I had to deal with things I didn't see other kids dealing with. For example, in Chicago, it was seven of us in a two-bedroom house. In Connersville, I wore soccer cleats to school because we couldn't afford shoes and cleats at the same time. Doing things that the other kids didn't have to do made me feel negative feelings. I would get angry, then when I cooled off, I would feel the darkness. I needed a change.

Being an angry kid, I let the problems build in my mind and would handle them in unhealthy ways.

When you're angry, society expects you to keep a straight mind and just get over it. That is not an option for a lot of people. Luckily, I found a way to break those chains. My change was boxing.

Boxing helps me in more ways than in the sport itself. It helps all aspects of my life just thrive. It makes me want to care for my body, my mind, my grades, and my relationships. It helped me change my angry tendencies. It helped me cut off the link from anger to depression and focus that anger into something productive.

After my first loss, I found out that sitting there did nothing for me. I came back and started improving more than I ever had. In a way, I fell in love with getting my ass kicked. It helps me see my flaws. It gives me things to work on and improve. If I have the drive to bring my desire to light, nothing can stop that.

I have goals of not just being a great boxer but being a great father and husband too. To do that, I can't let my anger spiral into depression like it has.

You can't always be in control of your anger and depression. More times than not, they probably are. It's how you react and channel your feelings that defines you. It is how you pull away from the darkness and find the light.

The thing you can control... the thing you have to control is that you never give up until you find it. The light is always worth that struggle in the dark.

CHAPTER 15: AN UPROOTED SEED OF DOUBT

APSARA SAKBUN'S STORY AS TOLD TO JOSEPH THOMAS

Key Words: Female, Collegiate-Women's Swimming, Athlete, Poverty/Race, Indiana

To be honest, I was not the most talented swimmer in the bunch when I first started swimming. Consistently, I was a step behind at swim lessons as I would watch my friends advance to the next group without me. I never took it to heart because I started swimming a little later than most of my swim mates, and swimming wasn't my main sport at the time. The simple fact that I was a child masked my ability to understand the social hierarchy within sports themselves.

My mother is Jamaican, and my father is Cambodian, so the culture within our house differed from my swim mates as well.

Seemingly every other day, I remember being asked, "What are you?" referring to my ethnicity.

While my teammates meant no harm, it gets rather tiring having to answer questions to make them feel comfortable with my mere presence. There were times I felt the pressure of being different, but I had to get accustomed to it if I wanted to take my swimming career to the collegiate level.

Most minority households don't turn their children's attention toward swimming, but my family seemingly took the unconventional route. As I got older, I began piecing together the demographic puzzle that is a swim team and started realizing why I was typically the only person of color in the pool.

Joining a swimming club typically costs more than joining a basketball or softball team, and the overall stigma about swimming in the Black community is rather negative.

This negativity stems from centuries-old limited access to swimming opportunities. Jim Crow laws saw Black people restricted from beach access until the mid-to-late 1960s. To put it simply, Black people just don't see many other Black people swimming at most levels, competitive or recreational; therefore, it won't be a part of the culture that is being African-American.

As I gained more experienced in and out of the pool, I began to teach swim lessons. Most of the kids I would teach were Black to my initial surprise and mostly because I lived in a fairly urban area. Despite that fact, most of the Black kids were there because their parents or school requirements forced them. Rarely were Black kids there for more intermediate levels for fun. These factors taught me to take pride in inspiring local Black and brown kids to at least try swimming through organized means. While I started to understand why there weren't many African-American swimmers, seeing Olympic-level swimmers like Simone Manuel and Cullen Jones gave me a sense of comfort going into the future. Manuel became the first Black woman to win an individual Olympic gold in 2016 in Rio de Janeiro, and Jones still holds the world record in the 4x100m Freestyle in 2008.

Outside of the pool, I've consistently felt balanced socially and academically. Going to public school in elementary school offered a welcoming feeling seeing people from a diverse array of backgrounds and cultures. In middle school, I saw myself surrounded by people from similar social classes and tax brackets in my classes. There were a few other Black and brown students like myself, but some of my white peers were quick to point out the acquisition of government aid to be able to attend the school.

While my white classmates showed their elitist tendencies, I slowly started to recognize my privilege as a Catholic school student, but I didn't realize it was privilege at the time. The innocence of my youth hindered my ability to understand the in-depth nature of these social constructs until high school. Ultimately, access to resources and the quality of the education differs heavily from public schools, and I was privileged enough to experience both settings.

While understanding negative, external factors such as socioeconomic and racial injustices and their impact on my potential in the pool, I had a good idea of what to expect in college socially and athletically.

My coaches and teammates at Ball State University try as hard as they can to make every athlete feel respected and part of the team. With the Black Lives Matter protests during quarantine summer, I saw my head coach, J. Agnew, as well as my conditioning coach, Mandy Harrison, and many others from the Athletic Department.

Seeing people who don't look like me racially but voicing their support of who I am as a human goes so much deeper than sports. Giving athletes of color a platform to perform without having to worry about external factors creates a true, level playing field.

However, the more I grew as an athlete physically and mentally, the more sly, subtle comments I would catch from my teammates. For example, my freshman year of high school, I got moved up to the anchor for the 200m Free relay. Being a freshman on a relay with three juniors was intimidating itself, but my three teammates gave me an especially hard time. Specific emphasis on words like "*my* 200 relay" from upperclassmen had me initially timid in my approach toward gaining team chemistry. Some subliminal comments may or may not have been racially motivated, but they certainly had me doubting my place in the swim community.

Added pressure came from feeling like I represented both Asian and African Americans because for a good amount of my teammates, I would be their closest interaction with a person of color to that point in our young lives. It took me so long to get very good at swimming, so I can understandably see where the doubt from outsiders came into play. On the other hand, a lot of swimmers peak in high school and make it to state consistently, which gave me a reason to not doubt myself because I knew it was only a matter of time before I saw exponential growth in the pool. When high school was said and done, I proved myself as one of the best swimmers on the team, considering that I swam at the IHSAA state every year, so if there was any further animosity toward me, I could have a good indication whether said animosity was race-related or not.

I didn't wake up one day and magically become a collegiate swimmer. It took ups and downs like every athlete, and yes, there were doubts because I saw how talented some of my peers were.

My older brother, Brandon, had a similar swim path as myself as he was a late bloomer too. Seeing his mistakes in the pool and learning from them helped me grow exponentially as alluded to earlier. Luckily, my parents were my biggest fans and inspired me to keep pushing. They laid a solid foundation for me and taught me how to expel mental and physical negativity into positivity. My parents' modesty will always ensure my ability to focus on my future and my swimming.

Chapter 16: A White Man's Game

Zyon Avery's Story as Told to Madi Jenkins

Key Words: Male, Collegiate-Baseball, Athlete, Race,
Indiana/Ohio/Florida

For as long as I can remember, I have always strived to be different. I wanted to stand out and make a name for myself. Sports seemed like a no-brainer. Growing up, it seemed like the most logical choice was to play football or basketball. That's what everyone around me played, but again, I wanted to be different.

Baseball gave me the opportunity to be different.

It seemed as if something was always in my way when it came to playing baseball. Growing up, the kids around me all thought I was stupid for trying to play a sport where I was the only individual who looked like myself. I was stupid for being a Black man playing the white man's game. Luckily, I had my family supporting me through it all. My father never let the words of others get in my head; instead, he pushed me to be the best ballplayer I could possibly be. But sometimes it seemed as if my best was not enough — even when statistically I was the best.

After a while, it becomes tiresome to never get fully recognized for my talents. The things I used to hear from my peers when I was younger started to creep back into my brain. I can still remember being in middle school and walking to practice at the end of the day with my equipment draped over my shoulder. Excited for practice. Excited to play the game I loved.

When a group of kids walked past and began laughing at me.

"Aren't big, Black kids like you supposed to play football?"

My father's words of encouragement came back in my head. I know who I am. It's easy now to look back and see those kids were just fueled by ignorance. Being a Black man in a white man's game. They only saw me for the color of my skin. Not who I really was.

It is easy now to look back and laugh at that situation.

But I did not want to be the same as everyone else. It's normal to see a 6-foot-2-inch, 225-pound Black man in football. I did not want to be normal. I did not want to ignore the stereotype that can be put on men in baseball — that they are all white, privileged, and just simply their overall build. I don't look like the stereotypical ballplayer, but I wanted to break that stereotype.

I graduated from a large high school in central Indianapolis. Around 1,000 other students in just my graduating class. It was easy to get lost in the crowd. Especially when the school is primarily a football school. No one really talks about baseball; it got pushed to the side. But I refused to be overlooked. I pushed every day.

I ended up becoming the first All-State baseball player my high school had seen in 36 years.

I was named All-County and All-Conference: a perfect game All-American. A four-year varsity-letter athlete, and I led my team as captain for three years. Essentially, I was not only just one of the top baseball players in my school but in my conference, county, and state, being ranked as the No. 2 catcher in Indiana. But also getting chosen as one of the top players in the country, getting the chance to enter my senior year being named as an Under Armour Preseason All-American athlete.

I had the credentials. Yet still would fall short in the eyes of others.

It is disheartening to know that even when I am at my best, I can still get overlooked because of how I look or what I represent. A Black man in America. I was a Black man playing the game of baseball. It was easy to say that I was noticed at my sport, but I would not necessarily say I was recognized.

It felt as if the attention was always on me. But negative. Like a target on my back. People watching and waiting to see if I would fail.

In my senior year of high school, I was privileged enough to have the opportunity to be a part of the All-State Team, but I was on the second team, an honorable mention. The person who ended up taking the place as the catcher on the first team did not have as good stats as me. It was evident to everyone that I was the only one who really deserved that spot. But no one wanted to talk about why I was not given that spot. I was better: My numbers proved it; my achievements proved it, but I did not look like the rest of the guys on the team.

I have to work even harder than those around me because of the color of my skin.

Sometimes it feels as if this won't ever escape me. The feeling of always feeling as if I am overlooked because of my skin color and not taken seriously because of my talent.

Opportunities are harder to come by. After graduating from high school, I was offered a Division 1 scholarship to Ohio University. I was blessed to have gotten this offer, especially since my end goal with baseball is ultimately to become a professional baseball player. But after spending two years at Ohio University, I began to realize that I was again being overlooked. Nothing was pushing me to make me become a better player. The opportunities weren't coming to me as easily as they were for other players. After a talk with my family, I decided it was best for me to leave Ohio and open my options to other schools.

No matter where I go, it seems as if I cannot be my true, authentic self. I always have to worry about what I do, what I say, and how I say things because of the color of my skin. Always struggling to try to fit into the environment around me.

It should not have to be this way.

Why do athletes have to conform when the sports teams themselves should be working hard to be inclusive to all? At times, it becomes hard to try and play for these fans and teammates who may never support who I am. I have to always persevere the challenges placed on me.

Baseball may be America's favorite pastime, but baseball doesn't seem to favor the Black man. Baseball is a white man's sport, funded by white men and supported by white men. So, it is only natural that they will want to see white men thriving in the sport and leaving the rest of us in the dust.

I do wish there were more representation in this sport. We have influential players like Jackie Robinson and Brandon Phillips, and these men mean a lot to players like me. But I feel that if we gave baseball players and the game more respect in our community — like how we idealize football and basketball in the hip-hop culture — more young men would want to participate and be engaged with the sport like how I am.

Baseball has always been a dream for me. I just want to play the sport I love, and finally, I want to believe I will be able to do that without feeling as if there is a color barrier in the way.

I was recently granted another baseball scholarship at Bethune-Cookman University. This University is not just a University to me. It already feels like home to me. Being able to attend a Historically Black College/University has always been a dream of mine. Knowing that I'll be able to attend an institution that accepts me for who I am and what I look like means that I'll no longer feel as if I am seen as less than because of something over which I have no control.

CHAPTER 17: TRYING TO FIND A PIECE OF HOME

MASHA POLISCHUK'S STORY AS TOLD TO PHILIP CHOROSER

Key Words: Female, Collegiate Women's Tennis, Athlete, International-Student Rights, Indiana/ (International) Russia

When I first got to the U.S., I thought my English was pretty good. But I got here, and I still had this language barrier.

I was like, "Oh, if we talk about something specific, I realized that maybe I don't really know English that well." Like, if we're at the gym, I'm like, "How can I say 'treadmill?" Or "How can I say 'lifting weights and stuff?'" So, for the past year, my English has definitely improved. I'm really glad that I'm learning and hope that it keeps getting better.

Coming from Russia, I was in a mixed-language school, but we still had most of our classes in Russian, so I was never really focused on English. I learned some English from school but mostly from traveling around for tennis. In my classes, it hasn't been an issue. But it was for one of my friends. English is her second language too, and she told a professor that it was really hard to understand the material in English and asked what she should do. He allowed her to use a translator for her work. But I guess that's it. Use a translator and hope that your teacher is fine with it.

There is a lot more responsibility here playing tennis.

Back home, there are no high school teams, so you're kind of on your own. Here, I am not doing it for myself. I'm representing my school and representing my team. There are 10 of us, so we're kind of like a unit where you have to keep maintaining this system and work together as a team. I have to push myself to work harder here because I'm not just playing for myself. And, yeah, I feel like we're practicing here more than I used to do in Russia. But I don't mind, and I feel like my tennis has improved, so harder is OK.

People don't understand how difficult life is as an international student-athlete.

The big one is how hard it is to be that far away from your home and be in, like, a completely new environment. I feel like some people don't realize how different the world is and that it is bigger than just what they know. Like, the culture is totally different. Attitudes are totally different. The world is big and can be very different with a different mentality.

I don't get to go home very often. Usually it's only during the summer. Our visa situation is a bit different. Most places you get your visa for four years. In Russia, you only get it for one year. So you either get it for one year and have to go back every year to renew it, or you get your visa for one year and just stay in the U.S. for the entire time period of your education. If I did that, then I wouldn't be able to go back to see my family for four years. There are really few appointments to renew it, and you can't do it in Russia. So, it's a really long and complicated process with lots of paperwork.

It also means even less time to see my family and friends. My parents live in Siberia, and that's about a 12-hour difference. And my sisters and friends, they're living in Moscow, and it's, like, eight hours, so I can only talk to my friends, like, in the first half of the day, which is sometimes kind of annoying because I have classes and I have practice at the only time when I can talk to them.

There also isn't much of Russia here in Muncie.

I have a Russian friend here, and almost every day, we're like, "Oh my God! I wish I could have this or this." We have a lot of, like, traditional Russian food, and, obviously, here you can't get it. The food here is really, really different. There are actually a lot of foods that I miss that I wish I could have. Here, it's so much more junk food. I'm used to eating more plain food and healthier than I do here, and, especially freshman year, when I was in the dorms and I had to go to the dining halls, it was a lot of junk food, and I was like, "Oh my God!" So much of the food is really deep fried or has so much added sugar. I just wanted some healthy options.

The thing that people need to understand is that international people need a lot of support for their first few months here. You are leaving your friends, leaving everything you are used to and moving far away.

Just showing you around. I never came on a visit, so I didn't know where things were. Helping you to meet new people. It's a different mentality and a different culture. Even giving little tips of advice and explaining the "rules" here of how to get along helps. I know a lot more now, and now I can help other international students in the future.

CHAPTER 18: COMING OUT AND INTO THE POOL

JACKSON KETCHAM'S STORY AS TOLD TO TANNER MARTELLO

Key Words: Male, Collegiate-Men's Swimming, Athlete, LGBTQ+ Rights, Indiana

I was not like every other guy at that age. It wasn't like the 1970s or 1980s where it was still taboo, but it was still definitely not as accepted or widely talked about at the time like it is today.

I first told my best friend, Michaela, who was on the swim team with me, and I first told her I was bi because I thought girls were pretty but I also thought I might like guys. So I told her and started slowly telling more of my friends, and it wasn't until later when I actually told my family.

I never had the full-on coming-out moment because when I told more of my friends, they ended up telling other people. I'm from a small town, so it got around the school pretty fast, and everyone knew about it. This girl at my school found out and ended up telling my brother, and he told my mom. That was a scary moment for me because I feel this process is something you figure out behind closed doors, and it's very private.

This felt like my make-or-break moment in life.

You see in the media stories about families kicking out their children for being gay or sending them to conversion-therapy camps. So, in that moment, I thought it would either end up really well or end up going very south. I know from other people's experiences — even people with progressive parents in general and parents who are openly pro LGBTQIA+ (Lesbian, Gay, Bisexual, Transgender, Queer, Intersexual, and Asexual) — they still tend to struggle with the coming-out process.

I was kind of just holding my breath, waiting to see what my mom's reaction was going to be.

My mom actually came up to me when we were on a family camping trip and basically said, "Someone is telling me you're gay. Is that true?" And so we had a little heart to heart, and I said that I'm gay and that I'd known for a bit. It was a weird experience because I didn't have the opportunity to sit down and actually tell them. It was brought to their attention by my brother.

I realized I was gay maybe around 12 years old. I knew something was different, although I didn't really know what gay was or if I was gay. I just knew that I was not like every other guy at that age. But it didn't take much longer for me to fully figure it out.

When I first realized that something was going on, for me, luckily, I had the Internet, so I was able to look up and explore what other people were talking about — like what gay is and what those feelings sort of meant.

From my perspective, it was uncommon being gay, especially growing up in a small town. You didn't know or hear about anyone being gay. It was kind of a quick connection, but I didn't realize how big of a deal it would have been or how rare being gay was at the time.

Growing up, we had sex education in my school: a little bit in middle school and then had to take a health course in high school. The classes were all very heteronormative courses where, obviously, you learn about teen pregnancy, STDs, and all that stuff.

But there are specific risks that queer people face exponentially as opposed to straight people.

So, if you're a part of the LGBTQIA+ culture and have unprotected sex, then you have a higher risk of STDs, drug use, and everything is just so much more heightened, which was never taught to us in school. HIV is one of the bigger risks for queer sex, but some people don't know that they can get HIV even though they are straight. I grew up never knowing about it because it was never taught to me, so you can't really blame some people because that's what they were taught. They were taught or made to believe that HIV can only be transmitted from a gay person. I mean, I had to do a lot of research on my own free time, and I'm hoping that the public's knowledge and understanding about this can expand in due time.

The first time that I knew there was any sort of discrimination toward LGBTQIA+ people in the medical field was when I was part of student council in high school. My school wanted to do a blood drive. I did my research to learn about Red Cross, and after my research, I personally did not want to hold a blood drive. I would not be able to donate blood because of their ridiculous standards for donations.

If you are straight, you are able to donate blood no problem. I know in the past if you were gay, you couldn't have protected or unprotected sex for a whole year before you could donate blood. The FDA revised the guidelines and changed it from 12 months down to 3 months.

Still, this is something I hope to further address while in the medical field.

Currently, I am on the swim team at Ball State University, and my team has been absolutely amazing to me. They are fine with me being gay and have not made me feel the slightest bit uncomfortable around any of them. Even with the swimming aspects — like you're in a tight, little speedo, and you have to change two-to-three times a day in the locker room. They have not pushed any stereotypical stuff on me, and I greatly appreciate that.

By contrast, in high school, people were a little more blunt with how they felt about me. I was never bullied or anything like that, but there'd been a few insensitive comments made toward me. I had people come up to me and say, "Don't look at me when we're in the locker room," and "I'm not comfortable around you." I know if I wasn't gay then I wouldn't have received those comments and all the other stereotypical stuff that gets pushed onto me. Stereotypical things that gay men face like being considered feminine or less of a man compared to straight people, or in sports, we can be made to seem as though we can't perform or compete as well as straight athletes.

I am my own person and want to be treated with respect.

I feel like respect is equal to validity. When people have an appreciation for what you do or for who you are. That my effort and achievements are acknowledged because of the hard work that I put in. What I accomplished is valid and not invalidated just because I am gay.

I do think that we are working toward a more accepting world for LGBTQIA+ people.

I already talked about my high school experience, and I'm hoping kids don't have to wait until college to be treated with the respect they deserve. You never know if one bad high-school experience is going to make them not want to go to college and pursue their dreams because they don't want to deal with the same discrimination in college that they endured in high school. I've told a lot of people that I feel like if I wasn't swimming and an MVP-point-getter for that team, then I would have received a lot more hate and discrimination. In other words, my athlete status made me an exception in others' eyes.

An MVP-point-getter is in reference to me being a top scorer and performing well for my team. For example, if you finished in 1st place, then you would receive 6 points; 2nd place is 4 points; 3rd place is 2 points, and so on. At the end of the season, your team would tally up all the points you accumulated over the year.

I just felt that since I was good at swimming, people were more willing to look past things that they viewed or perceived as flaws. I feel if I did receive more hate, then I would not have been thinking about going to college. I am grateful that I am going to college and use that as a big motivator to help others like me and change the perspective people have on the LGBTQIA+ community.

I am currently a nursing major and, unfortunately, there are not a lot of opportunities for me to teach others about these issues. But once I further advance in my nursing major and start working in the field, then I would like to inform and show people that sex education and healthcare is more than just the heteronormative narrative. Right now, I need to continue being a good student and further prepare myself so once I graduate, I can be ready to make the medical field more LGBTQIA+ positive and welcoming.

CHAPTER 19: JUST A BAT(TER)

KORBYN MCGOWAN'S STORY AS TOLD TO TYLER CASTLE

Key Words: Female, Collegiate-Softball, Athlete, Race, Iowa/Ohio

Family, friends, and teammates are what help me get through the hard times. My team can be like a second family, but what happens when that team doesn't treat me as one of them? As a biracial softball player, I've always felt like an outsider on every team. I hoped that was going to change when I was on my way to play softball collegiately. A racially diverse campus, an accepting team, and positive relationships with coaches were things I expected going into a collegiate sport.

However, I was very disappointed to learn that it was all a false reality that the university wanted me to believe.

The most important thing that drew me to play collegiate softball at this university was their claim of racial diversity. On day one, I realized how they used that to attract me to come to play for them. Upon getting to the university, I noticed that the diversity wasn't what they advertised. I realized that at the university there were only around 13 Black students. They used diversity as a tool to bring me into a school that they knew wasn't suited for what I expected. This immediately gave me bad vibes for how they created a false vision to lure me in.

When I went on campus tours, it always seemed to be on school breaks; specifically, they would bring me in during spring and summer breaks, which now seems very intentional. I believe they brought me in during breaks so I didn't realize the racial diversity didn't include Black students.

The athletic scouts knew that racial diversity was important to me, which included having other Black students on campus. We had discussions about diversity, and I was told over and over that I would be happy with the university's varied cultures. They used it to attract me to signing with them as a student-athlete. Signing with the school gave them my word that I would attend the university for school and for softball. I felt disrespect from the use of false diversity as a tool, but worse was the lack of respect for diversity on the team.

I hated the fact they used something so important to me to bring me onto the team, but even worse is when that team isn't sensitive to racism. One of my first experiences of being on the team started with a teammate using racial slurs. She was a white teammate who kept using the "n-word" in her everyday vocabulary. I asked her to stop but got the response, "My nephew is Black." I had no idea how to comprehend the idea of using racial slurs because she had a family member of the heritage. I didn't want it to be ongoing, so I decided to take the situation to my coach. The response I got was gut-wrenching. My coach went on to ask me things like, "Do you listen to music that uses that word?" Other things included, "Do you say that word yourself?" I couldn't believe that the coach was trying to defend my teammate by making excuses as to why they are using it. Nothing was done about this with my teammate, and it instantly distanced me from feeling like a family.

Teammates are supposed to be there for one another, and racial insensitivity wasn't something that I could take lightly.

Another unfortunate aspect of the team was having coaches whom I expected to understand my racial background but they didn't. They had already led me to believe that my racial experiences would be shared with other people on campus. Not only did I lose out on people to share my experiences with, but they also didn't understand how racial situations needed to be handled. I remember walking to practice one day when suddenly a truck started pulling up next to me. I was already nervous because I was walking alone in a town I wasn't very familiar with yet. He rolled his truck window down and started yelling racial slurs targeted at me. I was alone and had nothing to do about it, so I had to just keep heading to practice. When I got to the field, I was shaken up and broke down, starting to cry. I told a coach what happened, and all I could get was, "You're tough; it'll be okay."

I'm tough? How do I take that as empathizing with me?

I couldn't believe that I had to experience this around campus but also had to experience it independently.

It became even more apparent that the coaches didn't care about anything but the softball field. I shouldn't be going through these things on a "diverse" campus and especially shouldn't have coaches who don't care about the impacts of racist acts.

Diversity on a college campus should be an experience of multiple cultures and races that can empathize and share.

Unfortunately, I got the wrong end of that experience. This is an experience I believe a lot of kids go through when being recruited for collegiate athletics. I believe that collegiate sports should be all-inclusive with recruiters who are real about their universities. In the future, I hope to see softball and all sports recruit minority races with a real promise of racial diversity on their campus. Collegiate athletes need to feel welcomed and safe in their environment.

Ultimately, I decided to leave that team and university to pursue an environment where I felt more comfortable. I would advise any college athlete who doesn't feel safe or comfortable to do the same. I'm not a tool to build their athletic teams. I'm a minority student-athlete trying to find my place and to prosper in this world that doesn't always include me.

CHAPTER 20: DEDICATION AND STRUGGLE

JULIAN MCBRIDE'S STORY AS TOLD TO CALEB ANGLIN

Key Words: Male, Collegiate-Football, Athlete, Race, Indiana/Missouri

I cannot thank my parents enough. Their hard work cannot and will not go to waste. They gave me a life they did not have. They would not let my siblings and me struggle like they did when they grew up. From having no money and no food in the house, my parents have come a long way. They taught me a lot about how to be a successful Black American in the society we live in. They showed me that I need to get an education and that I can do anything I set my mind to.

It isn't always that easy though.

Throughout the past few years, there have been many riots, and they have brought bad attention to the Black Lives Matter movement. I am very grateful to be able to say that the Ball State University football team has made a positive impact in the locker room when it comes to spreading the word on the movement. Whether it is from sharing our stories to our teammates or talking to the community, we play our part and try to create change.

It is extremely important for us as athletes to use our platform to voice change.

Be the voice for people who do not feel comfortable speaking out and back the ones who continue to speak up. It is not only important to me but to many people on the Ball State football team and people in the Muncie community. We went around the community and shared our stories as well as shared our stories to one another during team meetings.

For example, the whole team had a part of Fall Camp called "Drivers." This was where every individual on the team would share what drives them to be the best version of themselves. Mine was my parents. They drive me every single day to be the best Julian I can be.

Something else that drives me is people doubting me. I went to prep school my junior and senior year of high school, and there was a coach who constantly put me down. He said I would never be a D1 athlete, and ever since that day, I try to be the best I can be on and off the football field. People like that coach, who said I would not be anything, have driven me every single day.

Being the best version of myself means that I strive to be a good person and do my best at whatever task is at hand.

Being a minority has not only affected us as a society, but it has also affected me in public school. I felt uncomfortable because of all the cliques and groups that were formed that did not involve me. Eventually, I moved to a prep school in Missouri during my junior year where I felt comfortable, and it was not as divided. The football team at Chaminade College Prep made sure to preach Brotherhood. That has stayed with me still to this day.

Brotherhood is extremely valuable, and it helped me feel the most comfortable I have ever felt. For example, when I made my official visit to Ball State, I felt extremely welcomed and like I was family as soon as I walked in the door. Head Coach Mike Neu has gone out of his way to make every player on the team feel this way. It was not just because I was a freshman either. He continues it to this day. For example, he invited all the guys from my freshman class over to his house for a cookout, and before and after every team meeting, he gives every single player a fist bump. He wants the best out of us, and he knows how great we all are. He cares about his players more than any coach I have ever had. He has become a father figure to many of us on the team.

One thing that will always stand out to me is when Coach Neu took some of the players on the football team to the BLM protests on campus. Along with that, there were a few spokespeople who came to the practice facility and went to an elementary school in Muncie. One man who spoke to the team was Brandon Martin, a fellow Ball State Cardinal. He was a great locker-room leader, a great football player, but he's an even better person, and you can tell that just by hearing him speak to the team. He was so passionate about the movement and sharing his experiences, and I remember that really opened some eyes in the locker room.

In 2020, my freshman year and the year that the coronavirus and the BLM movement really exploded, it was a standout year for our football program. We ended up winning the MAC title and upset the No. 19-ranked team in the nation, the San Jose State Spartans, 34-13 in the Arizona Bowl. It was not easy though. Our team had to overcome a lot. Not only with COVID-19, but since much of our school and team is very diverse, we had our backs against the wall all season. How the world was operating during that time made it extremely hard to focus on our craft. With everything going on in our society, sometimes it was difficult to focus on football, but the team stayed strong and got the job done.

The movements and protests in the Muncie community were all effective, but we felt that we were in a battle both on and off the football field. Again, the whole coaching staff and all our teammates being supportive helped a lot throughout the entire season by sharing personal stories in the locker room, talking to the community, and just being there for each other. It was an uphill battle in games and outside of the game, but we fought through it and defied the odds. At the end of the day, I think change will not and cannot be made unless we stand up for ourselves and fight for what we believe in.

CHAPTER 21: BEHIND THE 8-BALL

BRYCE COSBY'S STORY AS TOLD TO CHARLIE DESADIER

Key Words: Male, Collegiate-Football, Athlete, Race, Indiana/Kentucky

I saw a picture on Twitter once of what looked like a track meet. The art featured two people lining up to race with the final destination obviously being at the end of the track. But this wasn't your ordinary 4x4. On one end, the caricature had a clear, straightaway path while the other was faced with hurdles, rocks, and brick walls separating him from the finish line.

Man, this is what it's like to be Black in America.

As a human race, from the time we depart from our mother's womb, we are stamped. But the stamp on my skin is different. I learned that as a child when "the talk" featured my parents coaching me on what to do and what NOT to do if I was ever pulled over by the police to ensure that my chances of becoming another headline would be lowered. No guarantees on that, though. The stamp that has been placed on me is one that I will never be able to escape from — nor will I ever try to.

If I lost you, or if you don't get my drift: being born Black.

The melanin in my skin — that I had no say over — comes with a cost. Sometimes a deadly one. To be Black is to live with labels that you seldom live up to: being perceived as a threat, as violent, and as lazy. Black women punished with the stereotype of being loud and confrontational because of what is portrayed on television screens across the nation.

It's a constant, *constant* battle to withstand this image and to hold off this perception just so you can avoid being stereotyped. What makes it even harder is that there is zero room for error. We don't get to make mistakes because in this system — excuse me, in "our" system, it can cost you. Big time. Having to move through life with caution and awareness that you are different because of the color of your skin makes you feel like you're behind the 8-ball from birth.

Growing up as an athlete in Louisville, Kentucky, I had the best of both worlds. I was cool with the white kids, Hispanics, Blacks, Asians, you name it. But while we all accepted one another in our many different forms, family members of my peers weren't always on the same page. It wasn't until I was 9 years old when a sudden incident occurred when my white, childhood-friend's mother came out yelling at me to "get the f*** off of my lawn," proceeding to threaten to shoot me if I came back.

As young men and women of color, it's us versus the steel metal of a gun before we even learn to drive a car.

Trayvon Martin was the first time I had ever witnessed racial injustice. A kid who lost his life all because he was stereotyped. Fast-forward to the summer of 2020, and it was like reliving that trauma all over again. Following the death of Breonna Taylor, I protested with my people, fighting a fight that had never been won before and, in the end, still wasn't.

As athletes, sometimes we can feel that our voice isn't as powerful as people make it out to be and that our words don't hold much weight. But, you know, this is far from the truth. Hence why people are constantly telling LeBron James and other athletes to "shut up and dribble" or "stick to sports."

For me, it's always been about understanding the platform and that we *do* have a voice. All it takes is to impact one person. If we can impact one person, that's a step in the right direction.

If I gave a speech in front of 500 people, chances are maybe 497 won't care to listen. The message may go through one ear and out of the other. But for those three who were inspired and the message might have hit home for them, it could go as far as changing their life. Who knows what those three people could turn into just because of something that I said.

As athletes, I feel it is our duty — our obligation to God himself — to speak up and speak about the elephant in the room dressed as racial injustice. To sit and let things go on and not use your platform to inform and stand up is a disservice to you as well as the people who support you every time you step onto that gridiron, that hardwood, or that field. It starts with using your voice, not being afraid to talk about these topics no matter what setting — whether it's the barbershop or a family event or even social media. Being that African Americans make up the majority of my team yet we are still the minority in America, it is my due diligence as a leader of my team to spread knowledge and inform the masses whether it be through social media or in team meetings.

8-ball. Behind the 8-ball is like saying we're about to race, but you get a 10-yard head start. The odds aren't in my favor from the get-go. The beauty of it all? When I look at the Black community, I look at a group of people who have been able to overcome adversity time and time again. By no means did we ask for this. I personally feel that we shouldn't have had to endure the battles that have come our way. But I stand firm in saying that nobody has overcome as much as my race, and I stand by that. Through it all, I try to look at the positive and realize that while we are behind the 8-ball, as a community, we haven't made any excuses. We ask for help; we try to shed light on a lot of situations, and at the end of the day, we keep pushing.

George Floyd. Sandra Bland. Ahmaud Arbery. Breonna Taylor. Trayvon Martin. And to all of the beautiful, Black lives that were taken too soon, we will continue to fight. We will continue to speak up and work diligently on your behalf to ensure that racial injustice will transition into racial justice being served.

SPONSORS

ABOUT THE FACING PROJECT

The Facing Project is a 501(c)(3) nonprofit that creates a more understanding and empathetic world through stories that inspire action. The organization provides tools and a platform for everyday individuals to share their stories, connect across differences, and begin conversations using their own narratives as a guide.

The Facing Project has engaged more than 7,500 volunteer storytellers, writers, and actors who have told more than 1,500 stories that have been used in grassroots movements, in schools, and in government to inform and inspire action.

In addition, stories from The Facing Project are published in books through The Facing Project Press and are regularly performed on The Facing Project Radio Show on NPR.

Learn more at facingproject.com.
Follow us on Twitter and Instagram @FacingProject,
and on Facebook at TheFacingProject.

CPSIA information can be obtained
at www.ICGtesting.com
Printed in the USA
JSHW012127190123
36538JS00001B/36